AN INTELLIGENT FIRE

[handwritten inscription:] With my warm respect + appreciation

[handwritten signature] March '91.

By the same author:

What on Earth Is This Kingdom? (Kingsway)
Gerald Quotes (Kingsway)
Divided We Stand? (Kingsway)
He Gives Us Signs (Hodder and Stoughton)

An Intelligent Fire

GERALD COATES

KINGSWAY PUBLICATIONS
EASTBOURNE

Cover design by W. James Hammond

British Library Cataloguing in Publication Data

Coates, Gerald
    An intelligent fire.
    1. Christian life. Biographies
    I. Title
    248.4092

ISBN 0–86065–860–0

Printed in Great Britain for
KINGSWAY PUBLICATIONS LTD
1 St Anne's Road, Eastbourne, E Sussex BN21 3UN by
Richard Clay Ltd, Bungay, Suffolk
Typeset by J&L Composition Ltd, Filey, North Yorkshire

Contents

With Thanks

Firstly, to those who have allowed their own personal stories to receive international exposure through this book. I am grateful for your co-operation and willingness to have formerly private events made known for the blessing of thousands.

Secondly, to my secretary, Amanda Collins, who has typed every word of this book—and who has gone through various drafts, corrections and additions. You'll never get bored working for me, Amanda!

Thirdly, to Steve Clifford and others who made valuable suggestions with regard to content, perspectives and style. You are all extremely valuable to me and I wouldn't be where I am today without you.

Lastly, and most importantly, to Anona, my best friend. She shares this story, our joys, privileges, disappointments and heartaches. I have no doubt I couldn't find a better friend and adviser. You have enriched my life more than you'll ever know.

All the people in this story exist. They have been called by their real names. Anyone objecting to this should remember that space in the book is on their side—and does not allow for the full story!

There are many destructive fires raging through-out the nations. There is only one purifying fire; whose light shows us the way forward. He is The Intelligent Fire.

G. C.

God makes his angels winds, and his servants flames of fire.

Hebrews 1:7 (GNB)

A writer is rarely so well inspired as when he talks about himself.

Anatole France

For several years, medical authorities were alarmed at the infant mortality rate in certain hospitals. Posters were displayed: 'The first year of your life could be the most dangerous.' A quick-witted passer-by added: 'The last is not exactly without its hazards!'

Chapter 1

The Beginning (1944–1956)

On this day in 1835, Andrew Carnegie, the industrialist and philanthropist, was born in Dublin. On the same date in 1881, it was the birth of the Italian Pope John XXIII. In 1926, author of *Spy Catcher*, Peter Wright, came into the world—who was later to be launched on to an unsuspecting spy network. The date? November 25th.

In 1944 at a hospital in Woking, Surrey, Evelyn Maud Coates gave birth to a son whom she and her husband named Gerald. I was named after my father George's brother who had died a few years previously of a mystery illness.

Philanthropists, popes and spies are rarely remembered for their beginnings. It is their endings that leave the greatest impression. Most people are remembered for the last few months of their lives. But beginnings are important. At such times it is, of course, impossible to determine what a child will become. As the years progress, innocence invariably turns to at least a measure of guilt and shame. Playfulness so easily develops into ruthlessness. Dependence on others often gives way to independence of spirit, arrogant opinionatedness and a life which, as one grows older, is spent covering one's tracks.

The philanthropist, Pope and spy could have had no idea in their formative years of either personal successes or failures. But all three were heavily influenced by this early period. Most of us are. While some draw on these years as a resource to encourage and enrich, others close the door on them, regarding them as the annual dustbins of experience.

I myself would remember these years with mixed feelings. There were many happy memories, a series of warm experiences, delightful moments, pleasures and comforts. But these would be intermingled with confusion and sadness as I emerged into adult life. Neither my mother nor father would be alive to share in my own family life or their son's well-being, failures and successes.

I was the first of three children. My father, George, was born and had lived in Middlesbrough. The son of working-class parents, barely out of his teens, he found himself in the Royal Artillery. It was a time when all eighteen-year-old men were conscripted into the armed forces. The regimental navy-blue tie with its jagged maroon stripes was something I played with as a small boy, along with a wide range of medals, military badges and photographs.

Halfway through the war Dad was stationed in Cobham, Surrey, twenty-two miles south-west of Westminster in the heart of London. It was there he met Evelyn, herself just out of her teen years. She had been born and was raised in this small town, which then numbered no more than six thousand souls.

After a brief courtship they had decided to marry.

After the war they set up home in a pleasant, tiny village outside Cobham, named Stoke D'Abernon where a new road had been built. It was oval in shape and private houses of varying sizes had been erected in the outer ring. The inner circle alternated between a few private houses and the majority—council homes.

The garden of 28 D'Abernon Drive, in which the three of us took up residence, was soon filled with pole trelliswork on which roses with wonderful colours, shapes and textures shed their fragrance. To me, flowers always seemed remarkable, even awe-inspiring. Those roses, tall chrysanthemums, dainty daffodils, and a varied assortment of flowers whose names I could never remember, kept me happy for days on end. On my fifth birthday I was given a brand-new bicycle, and frequently on Saturday mornings I would set off with my father and explore the surrounding countryside.

Cobham School had been built in the centre of town. The rambling Victorian monstrosity had—sadly— survived several wartime bombs. However, when it was time to begin my formal education, I was allocated to Fetcham Primary School, which was over two miles further away. The London Transport 462 bus could complete the journey in less than fifteen minutes with stops. Around five other children shared the same journey each morning and afternoon, Monday to Friday. But the little troop did not include my childhood pal and next-door neighbour, Bryan Price. He was sent in the other direction to Cobham School! Perhaps it was this absurd dichotomy that sowed the seeds of my intense impatience with red tape and bureaucracy in later years.

The only things I disliked at school, with a growing passion, were the meals. Everything seemed to have such an odd and peculiar taste. Most meals resembled the aerial view of a farmyard. It was around that time I was told about Jesus, the loaves and fishes and the massive crowd who were fed quite miraculously. I was convinced that if Jesus had handed out the lettuce and beetroot we suffered at school, the crowd would have dispersed almost immediately, thus saving him the energy of the miracle!

Family life was stable, if somewhat uneventful. My father worked in engineering, and was one of those at the forefront in the use of plastics. Well-designed lampshades appeared regularly throughout the house. As a result, it sometimes resembled a *Doctor Who* set. Dad also came up with designs for walk-in, head-and-shoulders plastic telephone kiosks.

But he was more concerned with self-fulfilment and pleasing his boss than with monetary gain. I would frequently hear Mum exclaim, 'You're a fool, George— can't you see they're using you?'

Mum was a very hard worker and kept the house clean and tidy, despite regular massive migraine attacks. Like many other mothers, her sense of responsibility to the family kept her busy both at home and in part-time jobs.

Like all children, I learnt that life could be very unfair. One of my friends seemed to have a string of bad luck. One day, running across the main Fetcham Road which we crossed regularly to get to school, Paul was involved in a head-on collision with a car. The sight of the dent, the broken teeth and the blood kept me in shock for quite a while. Hardly out of hospital, Paul then contracted polio and walked with a limp after that.

One of the major influences on my early life was the local Sunday School. Most children in the area went along. The actual work, the drawings, talks and lessons, were neither particularly exciting nor boring. But the Sunday School superintendent seemed to make the classes come alive. 'Sandy' was the first Sunday School head teacher I encountered—I liked him. On one occasion, when Sandy was sick, his wife took over and she was both pretty and good. Mr Mellor, who lived in Tilt Road, took over several years later, and was certainly more austere and less charismatic. Yet he was a man whose sincerity and faith were quite clear—though I didn't think in these terms then. But finely-honed logic is sometimes better shelved for finely-honed intuition.

I had not a clue as to who were simply religious church-goers and who had real faith. Many years later I discovered that there was a difference.

There were only a few things that boys of my age did that were worse than naughty. A stolen sixpence here, a well-aimed punch upon a temporarily hostile friend—that sort of thing, but that was all. But there was one thing that was to stand out for many years and cause shame and embarrassment.

A fine Sunday School teacher lived opposite the Sunday School—Stoke D'Abernon village hall rented for the occasion—in Station Road. She was hardworking, efficient and unmarried. Her genuine interest in us was obvious. In gratitude, we came up with the bright idea of buying her a present. It was nearing Christmas and while the motivation was to be applauded, the fact was, we had no cash.

But having decided, we told the teacher, 'We're going to buy you a really nice Christmas present, Miss.' Somewhat taken aback at such corporate generosity, she dutifully went off and purchased gifts for every single child in the class.

The Sunday before Christmas Day, the boys all received a selection of lead soldiers, horses and military equipment. The girls received dolls and soaps. What were we going to do? There was no money and no gift on the horizon. I had an idea. The class went back to number 28, grabbed a large Jaffa orange, wrapped it in some blue tissue paper that was lying around, lifted one of the many Christmas cards off the mantelpiece, cut it in half and wrote a little message on it to the teacher. Feeling somewhat relieved, we presented ourselves at the front door, proudly handing in the dismembered Christmas card and a sad-looking orange. The teacher couldn't hide her disappointment. I am convinced she went into her home and wept.

On the third Sunday of the month, the Sunday School 'went to church'. St Mary's Church, Stoke D'Abernon, is a most pleasing piece of Saxon and Roman architecture containing the oldest brass-rubbings in England and some very fine stained glass windows. Not that I knew the difference—but this was not an evangelical Anglican church. The vicar was later to go into print in the local newspaper saying that Billy Graham was the 'biggest load of rubbish' he had ever heard in forty-five minutes. He christened me when I was a few months old, expected to confirm me as a teenager and, when older, I often imagined that the vicar would like to bury me!

The fine credal statements and the doctrine contained within the hymnology nevertheless gave me a helpful picture and awareness of God—despite the bells and smells of the church. I never really liked the building, surrounded by the graveyards and plastered with plaques commemorating the dead. Death and a love for the past seemed to be the predominant force of church life.

There were to be several occasions when death or serious injury was to close in on me. The first started inconspicuously enough. It was a Saturday afternoon. It had been a good summer. There was a glut of fruit around at rock-bottom prices. With the intention of making jam, Mum had purchased a carrier bag full of bags containing plums. While she was out shopping in Cobham, Dad and I sat down and tucked in to loads of the sweet, juicy and somewhat overripe fruit. How many we worked through can't be remembered, but I seem to recall that several bags of the fruit disappeared, plum-stones and all!

Upon her return, Mum ranted at Dad because of the vast number of plums that had been eaten and the few stones that were left. I went to bed that night feeling a little queasy. I didn't leave that bed for three months. My condition, gastroenteritis, was critical. I was so ill that the medical authorities couldn't move me to hospital. Visitors were few and Mum cared for me as though I was an only child.

Halfway through the sickness my grandmother appeared with a large box. Inside was a wooden Noah's ark which looked like a crude oil container full of wonderful wooden lions, tigers, giraffes and rhinos, which occupied me for weeks. The annual Cobham fête presented it as the main raffle prize, but whoever won the raffle heard about my sickness and gave it to Gran. I never did find out who the kind donor was.

Perhaps that was when I began to pray. God? Yes, I believed in God, just as I believed in the Royal Family and the heroic deeds of the Lone Ranger and the 'Cisco Kid. I often looked up at the stars at night feeling, 'I don't quite belong here.' But I was unable to translate those strange feelings into a coherent pattern of thought or belief.

The years at primary school were about to finish and I sat the eleven-plus which I thought I might pass. I failed—quite spectacularly! At weekends I played in D'Abernon Drive, which was virtually free of traffic, and even did a little gardening every now and then, to the annoyance of my father! Sometimes the two events coincided when our football demolished a plot of specimen flowers being prepared for the Cobham garden fête!

I had already worked out that people are good at what they enjoy, and enjoy what they are good at. I never did work out which was the cause and which was the effect. Sport I didn't enjoy and wasn't good at. In school I was always the last choice in the football team ('Oh well, we'll have Coates, then'). Later, I read a playwright who commented, 'Football is all very well as a game for rough girls, but it is hardly suitable for delicate boys.' I agreed with him entirely and still do!

If the Royal Family and God existed, I wasn't at all sure about Father Christmas. Noddy and Big Ears could not possibly be real people. If they were, what were those dangling strings? Entering my parents' bedroom one day during the holiday period, I unlocked the wardrobe (without a key!) and inside found a pale-blue desk. 'Funny place for an office,' I thought to myself. Christmas was getting near.

I hid my tracks successfully. My parents never did discover my doubts until a heated debate took place between us three children.

'Oh, you don't really believe in Father Christmas!' I taunted my younger brother Roy and sister Miriam, with an air of superiority. Our parents realised I had been into the holy of holies—but they let it pass.

Something they didn't let pass was my unfortunate ability to pocket the occasional Mars bar, tube of Polos— or Rolos if I could—from the local sweet-shop. History was to be full of 'God exalting the humble', soon followed by 'How are the mighty fallen'. This humble little lad felt he was doing quite well, as the thieving was neither regular nor extensive. I even taught my mates how to nick a bar or two of something or other right under the noses of the shopkeepers, without them realising it. Unfortunately, the plain-clothes detective standing behind me on one occasion did realise it. I was sent home to get my father.

I stayed at home waiting for the Third World War. It wasn't the Third World War—it was Armageddon! My uncle and aunt just happened to be there. I got the hiding of my life, and the shame of being spanked in front of them was a far greater discipline than anything else my parents could have invented.

Despite the family having a car, the only long journey I remember was to Middlesbrough, an uncomfortable ride with five occupants. We stopped off late at night in days long before Kentucky Fried Chicken, McDonald's hamburgers or even Wimpy Bars. We purchased ham sandwiches from a mobile snack-bar, into which it seemed the entire output of Colman's mustard factory had been spread! Mum and Dad, along with son number one, resembled rockets leaving a silo!

Upon arrival, I found out that the reason for the long trip was the death of Dad's father. Grandad and Gran had a tiny terraced house in a street that looked identical to all the others. Not a tree in sight. The next day, I was taken to the sitting-room where the open coffin and the body of Grandad lay. It was a horrible experience; I had never seen a dead body before. Mum, somewhat predictably, along with Gran, spent the entire time cleaning the house from top to bottom, scrubbing floors, cleaning windows and erasing the appalling smell of cats that lingered everywhere.

The only other memorable trip was to the Farnborough Air Show with an aunt and uncle. I was far too small to see anything other than what zoomed overhead, or what appeared—or disappeared—at lightning speed. Occasionally I was allowed to sit on the shoulders of my uncle. I was never quite sure what I was looking at, as it seemed one needed actually to catch a plane ride to get where all the action was taking place! As the day drew to a close, I was aware that something unusual had happened. It was 1952, and a supersonic jet had disintegrated in mid-air, killing twenty-seven people on board.

I had a near disaster myself. The local recreation ground had a stream running through it. After a long, torrential downpour, it burst its banks and flooded. The bridge of railway sleepers was submerged. Endeavouring to cross it, I missed and was carried downstream. Just before I disappeared into a five-foot wide drain, I was rescued by a passing lady. This was the second time death nearly triumphed.

Despite its occasional shocks, life was fairly stable. But all that was about to change for ever. I was aware of a cousin named Ray. For some reason, I thought he was a distant cousin for no other reason than that he lived a long way away! In reality he lived in Cobham. But that was a long way away when you have usually travelled the other way to Fetcham by bus! There were the annual May celebrations on the Tilt Green, halfway between Cobham and Stoke D'Abernon. The day arrived, complete with maypole, morris dancers, lemonade and banana sandwiches—surely one of the worst inventions since beetroot! Other than on Mayday, I was rarely ever seen in Cobham.

So it was something of a shock to find that Ray had come from wherever he lived, appearing on our doorstep in the spring of 1956. Unknown to me, an American evangelist in his early thirties had appeared in Britain two years previously. He was just about to return and launch another national crusade. He later regretted ever leaving Britain after record crowds in England and Scotland brought him perhaps the nearest he had ever been to a religious revival.

The evangelist and I were to meet—but not for well over thirty years. At the same meeting, I was to receive an embrace, a punch on the arm and a 'Hiya, mate' from a friend recognised as Britain's best-known

Christian. He would be a rock-singer, but in 1956 hadn't started his career. The singer was to inform the British population about his new-found Christian faith in Earl's Court, at a massive rally the evangelist addressed in 1966.

But I was about to have a little revival all of my own. Not in Haringey, Kelvin Hall or Earl's Court, but in Coombe Bissett near Salisbury. Not in a building, but in an open field. Not with thousands of others, but virtually on my own. Ray was the link.

'The trouble with Born Again Christians is that they are an even bigger pain the second time around.'

Herb Caen

'If you will do right—God will see to it that you come out right.'

Anon

Chapter 2
The Turning (1956–1961)

'Gerald, come in here,' Mum called. 'Ray is here and wants to put something to you.' I had no idea of the reason for Ray's appearance in Stoke D'Abernon at this particular time.

As it turned out, Ray belonged to a club, where archery was the main sport. A group of local lads were going off to camp near Salisbury in Wiltshire. 'Well— would you like to go?' Mum asked.

'Yes, I think so,' I replied, somewhat gingerly, never having been away from home for more than forty-eight hours.

Within a few weeks, I waved goodbye to my chums at Fetcham Primary, none of whom I was to see again. One Saturday morning, my parents drove me to Old Common Road in Cobham, where a brown open-backed lorry took eight boys and our kit-bags to Woking Railway Station. Woking was to have a lot to answer for. British Railways took us on the next leg of our journey. Peering out of the train window, I saw the tall spire of Salisbury Cathedral and for some strange reason it gave me a sense of well-being.

A van took us from Salisbury Station to Coombe

Bissett. There we met the Lodge family, who owned and worked on Lower Pennings Farm. Spread across a field were large, round, brown canvas pancakes. 'These are bell tents,' an officious leader told us.

The sun was shining, and soon boys from various parts of Britain began to erect the tents. Inserting a large timber pole under the brown canvas pancake, a couple of lads struggled to lift the pole while others outside pulled on the guy-ropes. In what seemed to be no time at all, the site looked like an eighteenth-century army base, complete with a white first-aid tent and a larger marquee for meetings. A loud-mouthed cook was shouting in the kitchen, incessantly banging a triangle every time he made a meal or even a pot of tea!

If hell is unending loneliness, raw vulnerability, and not being taken notice of—the first week was hell. British Railways offered discounts to parties of eight or more, and this particular group from Cobham only had seven in their party—until Ray remembered his cousin! But there was something odd about the whole set-up. Despite rain everywhere, there was a comradeship, a definite 'in-the-know' club atmosphere I couldn't break into.

At the close of the first week, wet, muddled, hungry and uncomfortable, I decided to go home. The weather was so bad the entire camp was evacuated into nearby barns. I was moved with tears streaming down my face; I felt so isolated among so many people. Another week of this would be unbearable.

But eventually, a large orange ball appeared in the sky, the ground dried out very quickly, and 'normal' camp life began. There was breakfast in the open air, and lots of it as well. Visits to places of interest including Stonehenge, Salisbury Cathedral and the market-town itself soon banished homesickness. During the day there was archery and in the evenings, the boys gathered in the marquee and sang songs and somebody would tell a story. It wasn't always clear what the story was about, but somehow God came into it.

If you were 'converted', the camp leaders left you alone; but if you weren't converted, grown men in khaki shorts would sit down on a straw bale and ask, 'Do you love Jesus, young man?'

Even my tent leader, Mike, asked, 'Are you a Christian yet, Gerald?'

Shocked at this somewhat personal intrusion, I responded hesitantly, 'Ugh, oh yes!'

Tent leader Mike, probably displaying great discernment, enquired, 'And where did that take place?'

I was caught off balance. 'Oh—em—it happened at St Mary's Church in Stoke D'Abernon.' Mike seemed satisfied.

But there was another pressure, one I couldn't explain. Towards the end of the second week, when somebody in the marquee was telling their story, I felt distinctly uncomfortable. Somehow, I knew there was a God who loved me, who knew all about me and was actually looking for friendship with me. Such a notion seemed absurd. But in the non-religious atmosphere of the marquee, with straw bales and wooden planks, it somehow seemed so much more real and obvious than in an old musty building where most people only whispered and had developed a funny walk.

So God loved me! But what about the naughty things I'd done? I understood that Christ had lived the sort of life I should model my own on. Jesus, I had learned at Sunday School, was then killed. Easter was all about Jesus taking the punishment for all the wrong that people have done, a sort of substitute in the cosmic moral order of things. Now I was hearing that every wrong-doer who wanted to turn away from living a life without God could be forgiven, because Jesus had taken the punishment. Not only could they be forgiven, but made clean and receive the gift of the Holy Spirit.

On the one hand, it all seemed so incredibly reasonable and obvious. But on the other hand, I was haunted by the question of why nobody else had ever made this clear, either at home or Sunday School. I found it difficult to believe—but believed. I was finding out that in order to be elected one had to become a candidate. I could hardly cope with this new-found fortune.

That night, I walked back to our tent and told Mike I wanted to become a Christian.

'I thought you were,' Mike responded.

I was in a corner, and it wasn't to be the last time. 'Oh,' I mumbled, 'I don't think I did it properly.'

It was a simple affair. Mike, the tent leader, and the leader of the camp (Mr Good, I recall) asked if I really wanted to give my life to Christ. When I responded positively, albeit with embarrassment, they then prayed a prayer, line by line, which I followed out loud: 'Dear God in heaven, I thank you for Jesus, for his birth and his life, his death and his resurrection. Please forgive me for the wrong I have done, and for failing to do those things I should have done. I am sorry for my sin. I ask that you will cleanse me of my present condition, and fill me with the Holy Spirit. From this day forward, please make out of me what you want me to be.'

I was given some literature and some encouragement, and told I would enjoy the last few days at the camp more than all the rest put together. They were right. A flame had been lit from a Flame that made so much sense of me and of the way things are.

Someone read to me from the Bible, Romans 10:9: 'That if thou shalt confess with thy mouth the Lord Jesus, and shalt believe in thine heart that God hath raised him from the dead, thou shalt be saved.' True, it was the old-fashioned Authorised Version, but for all of its archaic language, I understood precisely what it meant.

The last few days sped by. I was so excited I couldn't wait to get home and tell my parents what had happened. The train whisked us back to Woking Railway Station, and there was the brown lorry to take us back to Gran. Her home was situated just off the A3. She had made a pot of tea for Mum, Dad, Roy and Miriam. They told me about their holidays, places they had been to and things they had done.

'And what did you do on your holiday?' Mum enquired. I had been prepared for this question.

'Well Mum, I have been born again, saved and converted!' The entire family froze for a moment, and looked as though they had just been told that I had brought a Martian home with me.

'That's nice,' Mum spluttered, busying herself with the tea and biscuits. She then went on to explain that she had my favourite steak and kidney pie in the oven waiting for us when we got back home.

I was somewhat bewildered. 'What's the matter with them—don't they understand? This is the greatest thing that has ever happened to me,' I thought. 'Here I am talking about God, salvation, a complete change of life on the inside, and here is Mum talking about a three-and-sixpenny Wall's steak and kidney pie in a tin!' I thought I'd give them time to come to terms with my new experience—but they were never to refer to the incident again.

Now aged nearly twelve, I had never heard of Victor Hugo, a French novelist who had died seventy-one years previously. It was he who wrote, 'Like the trampling of a mighty army, so is the force of an idea whose time has come.' I knew I had something more than an idea: I had received a Person whose ideas had changed history. I wasn't sure which parts of history or where the history took place—but I knew. At school I remembered that the pink bits on the map were the Christian bits—or were they the British bits? Or were they the same?

Although still young, I knew I had found a Person and an idea whose time had come. I still couldn't work out why my entire family didn't ask more questions, and why I couldn't lead them in a similar prayer. But a fire had been lit in my soul—one that would remain alight, though at times the flame would flicker. This burning flame would one day enable me, through modern communications technology, to lead almost 250,000 people across the United Kingdom in a prayer of commitment to this Person and this idea, and to reach the nation with the same gospel message 'over and over again' by the year 2000.

Although I had been processed through a religious system, this was something quite different. Coincidentally, perhaps due to peer pressure, it was around this time that I gave up on the Anglican Church. The reason had more to do with man (or boys, actually!) than God. We were never asked if we would like to go up into the next class of Sunday School. It was accepted that from one year to another, that is what would happen. But when we were eleven, the Sunday School became silly enough to give us that choice. Would we like to go to Bible Class? It was held over half a mile in the other direction. From a psychological point of view, for us, that was bad news. Few made the transition. My pals had decided that Sunday School and church were over for them, and I didn't want to go to a Bible Class all on my own! So the Anglicans waved good-bye to me, something for which most of their leaders are now profoundly thankful.

Not only did my parents not understand what had happened, but neither did new-found friends at Cobham Seconday School. Yes, I made it in the end and caught the 462 to go the other way—into Cobham. There had been a turning away from a vague religious faith to something—no Someone—specific and real. There had in a sense been a turning away from my parents, who had turned their back on my experience with a mild dose of apathy. Apathy is the vilest form of rejection. There was a turning away from the Anglican Church. I turned instead to a youth group which met weekly in a house in Canada Road, not far from Cobham High Street, and was led by an elderly man called Mr Jeffries. (We nicknamed him 'Judge'.)

A new school was being built just behind his house in Canada Road, on land adjoining the gun site which my father had been based on. But the building was behind schedule. The first year, I was educated in the Victorian dump which had escaped the bombs. In my second year, the school was still unfinished so I continued my education in a Nissen hut on the new school site.

Despite an average education, I was sent into the top level 'A' stream. I found it tough going. English, art, history, geography, music and religious knowledge I enjoyed with immense satisfaction. But maths, geometry, technical drawing, science and woodwork were studies I loathed—and they seemed to be the studies the teachers enjoyed.

Then there was sport-something which I was sure was demonised, even before I believed in demons! Most of the time, I either felt inadequate or intimidated, and hated being one of the last to be chosen to be in any team.

There was just one occasion when I did well. I was paired off with a nimble, muscular opponent in a boxing match. Usually the fight lasted about ten seconds, with me looking up at the opponent—about five feet up! Quite by accident, I placed my foot on my opponent's and the opposition, unable to step back, received a clout to the side of the head. The opponent was swiftly despatched to the floor before surprised teachers and onlookers. Unaware of what had really happened, my pals gave a rousing and astonished cheer at this newly-discovered skill. Unfortunately, it not only rocketed me to fame but rocketed me into the boxing-ring with the most proficient school boxers, who systematically pulped me silly before incredulous teachers and pupils. 'How are the mighty fallen' indeed!

One discovers a lot about oneself between the ages of twelve and seventeen. I now call these years 'the twilight zone'. I felt I was no good to God because I was too worldly, and no good to the world because I was too religious. That is a very lonely place to be. While grateful for my family, I felt they didn't understand me or my faith. But I went along to the weekly club and the annual camp, so my school-friends knew I was a Christian.

Although I was relatively happy at home and school, there was a sense of isolation at both. Continuing with education, I enjoyed the subjects I used to enjoy, but with more enjoyability! And I loathed the subjects I used to loath with greater loathing! Certain teachers I respected, especially a Mr Twinn who I later found out was a fellow-believer. Somehow, I was discovering the difference between the real and the unreal.

'Religion is the fashionable substitute for belief,' Oscar Wilde wrote in *The Picture of Dorian Gray*. I didn't like religion then, and it didn't like me. The school was a Church of England Secondary School. That didn't appear to mean much, other than that the vicar used to come and give little pep talks; he was quite a nice chap.

The one thing I did enjoy a great deal was music—I was later to bemoan the fact that I couldn't play an instrument. I often sat in music class working out what value there was in playing the piano, flute or guitar when grown-up. I couldn't see the point, so I didn't

learn an instrument. But the music and drama depart-
ments agreed to do a Gilbert and Sullivan operetta and I
was chosen to take part.

Starting with *The Mikado* (still considered by those
who can remember to be the best production the school
ever put on), I landed the part of Nanki Poo, the son of
the Mikado. 'A wandering minstrel I,' I sang, which
turned out to be strangely prophetic. In the middle of
rehearsals, my voice broke and the resonant tones could
be heard throughout the school, bringing teachers from
their classes down into the foyer of the building. Mrs
Barden, our music-teacher, encouraged me to continue
singing, and I was later chosen to be the judge in *Trial by
Jury* and the major-general in *The Pirates of Penzance*.
Some reckoned that the famous 'patter song' was the
basis of my machine-gun public oratory.

But I soon slipped from the 'A' stream down to the 'B'
stream, where I acknowledged, at least privately, I felt
more comfortable. I was nearly always at the top. Being
at the top of the 'B' stream was infinitely better than
being bottom of the 'A' stream. Although I excelled in a
few areas, I only ever passed one examination and that
was the CSE English examination—with credit. I never
took the GCE and became increasingly uninterested in
the educational system.

It was author, broadcaster and, later, acquaintance,
Malcolm Muggeridge, who summed up my teenage
feelings succinctly: 'The education system in this country
is like casting artificial pearls before real swine.'

I didn't have many close friends at school. Well, boys
don't, do they? With regard to sporting trophies and
academic flair, I did the school no favours. Perhaps the
one thing I might have done was to add a certain colour
to the school dramas and musical presentations.

Occasionally, pupils would come to me with their
problems, receiving advice and even a prayer or two. A

guy called Dave chose a career in the Royal Navy. It was a big decision. We talked, I advised and then prayed. I never did hear of him again! But as far as I know, he could still be sailing round the world.

There was another guy called Geoff. He was the school hunk. The girls were round him like bees round a honeypot. I didn't give him any advice—he gave me some. I had apparently been counselling one of his girlfriends (he had a few!), and he thought I was about to steal her. He waited for me outside school, tapped me on the shoulder, I turned round and he nearly knocked me into kingdom come! (And I don't even believe in dispensationalism.)

Future leadership skills were being developed. Fatherly, policeman-like talks were given as I rocked backwards and forwards on the ball and heel of my feet. The recipients of all this counsel may have thought I was a prize twerp, but maybe I was bringing a little bit of heaven to St Andrew's School. Interestingly, some of those children would go on to work with me thirty years later.

Only once was I disciplined, though I felt that the punishment was unfair on this particular occasion. Pupils had crowded into the dining-room for lunch, and there was louder clatter than normal. As the piglets waited for their lunch, one of the teaching staff called for silence. The noise was so great he couldn't be heard and our table was identified as the main culprit.

We were called out for a public demonstration of who was in charge. It clearly wasn't me or my pals. With a hall packed full of fearful onlookers, the eight members of the offending table were asked to put their hands out in a row while the teacher lifted the cane. Suddenly aware that nobody could get on with their meal, as grace had not been said, the teacher asked me to 'give thanks' for what we were 'about to receive'. I was then promptly thrashed with the cane!

Family life continued at a fairly peaceful and leisurely pace. Mum was still working as hard as ever, and was still suffering acute migraine attacks. Dad was content at being ripped-off at work, when Mum became suspicious. Asking for some extra housekeeping, she was told it wasn't possible.

'I don't know what you spend all your money on, George,' she retorted. She may not have known—but she probably guessed.

One day, I was helping Dad in the garden when some attention to the lawn-mower was needed. The brick-built shed, while loaded with tools and implements of all sorts, didn't contain the proper spanners. Remembering that some equipment was kept in the glove compartment of the car, I ambled out to the front of the house. I tried the driver's door, which was locked, and went round to the front passenger door. I turned the knob on the glove compartment and as I searched through some papers, out dropped a photograph of a bikini-clad woman. She bore about as much resemblance to my mother as *Top of the Pops'* Kylie Minogue does to *Neighbours'* Mrs Mangel.

Dad, looking up, saw me in the car and nearly soared through the ozone layer. He screamed words that were beyond definition, so I beat a hasty retreat, realising that something was seriously amiss.

While the relationship with my parents was not close, there was an absence of conflict. One notable exception was when I was going off to a meeting of the Christian youth group. A Bible was tucked under my arm. Mum, probably having had a bad day, was labouring under a double dose of recurring negativism—which had a debilitating effect on all that surrounded her.

Pointing to Miriam, who sat reading a spicy romantic novel, she shouted, 'Why don't you read something decent, like your sister!'

The absurdity of the scene eluded me at the time, though I laughed at it on many later occasions. It furthered my feelings of being misunderstood and even rejected. There were times when I wondered who in the family was going mad.

Every Friday, almost without fail, come hail or shine, I went to the youth group. It entailed a bus journey into Cobham or, when there was no pocket money left, a two-and-a-half-mile walk. Mr Jeffries was an old man, probably a bit odd, but there were wonderful qualities about him which we admired. I felt very much accepted by the group. During the winter months, Friday nights were filled with table games, a welcome break for drinks and biscuits, and a talk by Mr Jeffries which was always interesting. Summer months involved rifle shooting, archery, the occasional visit to a place of interest—but I never went to the Bible Class on a Sunday.

However, I was beginning to find things out about myself, and most of them I didn't like. One is not overtly conscious of wrong-doing at the age of eleven or even twelve in quite the same way as when one is seventeen or eighteen years old. One's responsibilities, and therefore moral choices, seem somewhat heightened in later teenage years. While character is revealed in great moments, it is made in a multitude of little ones. It was these little ones that bothered me. I found, for example, that I had an ability to tell a story that was not altogether true—and it didn't bother me. That's what bothered me!

Despite a near-public beating for stealing Rolos (which I would have happily shared with my best friend) I was beginning to steal again. It wasn't large amounts of money or anything like that, but I had taken a weekend job in a local confectioner's/coffee shop. It was not difficult to pocket a bar of chocolate or, if times were really hard, fail to ring up an item on the till.

Half the shop was devoted to sweets and tobacco, plus a few domestic items. The other section was separated into a cafeteria area. Behind the shop were the living quarters and behind them was the kitchen, which was used to prepare hot snacks and cream teas. Black and white gingham curtains hung on either side of the kitchen windows. Nearby was an Ascot water heater. In summer months, with gas ovens on, the windows would be open, allowing a cool breeze to flow through the entire area.

The owner would often come into the kitchen uttering, 'One day those black and white gingham curtains will get blown into that Ascot heater and this whole place will burn down.' This went on month after month, summer season after summer season.

So one day, I decided to help the curtains! The fatal words were uttered once more by the owner, who turned her back on the kitchen and returned to the shop. Bravely, I stuffed the curtains into the Ascot heater, turned the hot-water tap on, but was promptly called into the shop to help serve customers. Initially shocked and afraid of being discovered, I composed myself, but within ten minutes of serving customers and engaging in conversation, completely forgot what I had done.

The owner's daughter left serving customers some ten minutes later. 'Fire! Fire! Fire!' she shrieked, at the awful discovery. The proprietor and I ran to the kitchen. The whole place was alight. Wooden pelmets over the windows, the ceiling with its glossy paint peeling off, and even kitchen cupboards were all ablaze. But there were no more black and white gingham curtains!

At home Mum and Dad were settling into mediocrity; they were products of an age that had gone to war—and won. Their parental control was lessening considerably. Sunday School and church were now behind me, though my sister Miriam and brother Roy still attended.

At school I became assistant head boy and continued studies with mixed emotions and results. The Christian Archery Movement continued to meet weekly and camp annually. Every year a group from Cobham joined with a hundred other lads at Coombe Bissett. One of our major projects was to dig a swimming-pool next to the campsite. The year it was completed, the boys spent much of their free time pushing each other in and having a lot of fun.

One hot sunny day, I was standing by the deep end when two lads pushed me—not realising I couldn't swim. As I touched the bottom I went into a knees-bend position, jerking myself up and shooting vertically through the water. I gasped for air before going down to the bottom again. My pal Bryan Price saw what was happening. Diving in, he grabbed me and pulled me to the surface, spluttering and semi-conscious. But bravado forced me to close the door on the episode. No doctor was called and camp life continued. I have often wondered what would have happened if Bryan Price hadn't been around.

For a short while, due to peer pressure, I began to smoke cigarettes because 'I want to be a man'. A few months later, I gave up the ghastly habit, for the same reason!

But slowly I was becoming two people. Publicly, I was a model son, with average but creative abilities at school and in the uniformed youth movement. Privately, inner conflicts pulled and often won. The growing sense of 'being different' from others led me to look for acceptance in other areas. These were not good places.

In the next town, fellow-pupil Marc Bolan was em-
barking on a short-lived rock music career. In the next
road, Bob Willis was being groomed for international
cricket stardom. Occasionally I went to see Bob with
Bryan. My own career was not to last much longer than
Marc's or Bob's—but for different reasons.

The twilight zone continued and near-death was yet
again just around the corner. In specific though limited
ways, I would one day be able to foretell the future, but
I couldn't foretell my own. Turning to faith had already
engaged me in some battles—it was about to engage me
in some more.

Great people have purposes, small people mere wishes.
I wanted to be great. The next few years would determine whether I would follow the Intelligent Fire into
those purposes.

'The secret link between aspiration and achievement is development.'

G. C.

'More people would learn from their mistakes if they weren't so busy denying them.'

Harold J. Smith

Chapter 3

The Aspirer (1961–1967)

The flame of faith was still alive. Inner conflicts couldn't be denied but, lacking terms of reference, I didn't know whether these were normal. I stayed on at school for a while, more because of Gilbert and Sullivan than Einstein and Wordsworth. It was 1961 and I was almost seventeen years of age.

In answer to a newspaper advertisement, I visited nearby Epsom. A vacancy had occurred in the display team of a retail outlet, H. L. Reid & Co. It was situated next to the Spread Eagle hotel in the centre of town. The aging Victorian departmental store was to remain for another twenty-eight years before being demolished for a new shopping mall. The Spread Eagle was preserved and refurbished.

The four-floor store sold just about everything. The display team, led by the handsome, if at times irresponsible, Derek Horwood was in charge of newspaper advertising, special promotional events, interior displays, exhibitions and window presentations. I was offered the job and accepted.

The work was demanding but creatively rewarding. One promotion, advertising American merchandise, saw the General Manager, Mr Candy, clattering through Epsom High Street, resplendent in a stage coach and four with Red Indians in pursuit. Another exhibition of designer clothes took place on a ship. 'Anything not nailed down will disappear,' the display team were told. We took no notice. We never saw the clothes again.

The display studio was situated on the flat roof of the building, ensuring my slimline build for at least another nine years—the entire term at Epsom. Within four years of beginning my career, Derek Horwood left for Oxford Street. I probably became the youngest display manager for a departmental store on record. But four years is a long time, especially when you are just out of school.

One Christmas eve, seasonal decorations had given way to the inevitable sales signs for the January chaos. At the close of the day I dashed up onto the fourth floor for the ritual floor-by-floor inspection to be sure that Christmas was forgotten for another year and the splashes of red and white tickets and signs were everywhere. It was also a good opportunity of wishing staff a happy Christmas. Traditionally, departmental store staff hate the display department. They are a law unto themselves, never available when needed, have always got reasons for doing what everybody else wants to do but can't, and flaunt their freedom to the extreme annoyance of everybody else.

As I reached the fourth floor, I went into the restaurant to wish the chef and restaurant staff a happy Christmas.

'Come and have a drink with us, Gerry,' the chef shouted.

I didn't drink, in fact I'd never had a drink other than a secret shot of gin which my father kept in the drinks cupboard. It was awful. At home I was still Gerald, but for some strange reason from the day I started work I was Gerry and was so for the nine years I worked at H. L. Reid. Afraid I would miss the train, I grabbed the large tumbler, supposing it was full of wine. Hot and perspiring from the activity of the busiest day of the year, I downed the entire contents. But the wine was whisky!

To roars of laughter, I put down the glass and must have looked as though my head had been hit with a telegraph pole. 'Thanks a lot,' I laughed. 'Have a happy Christmas.' Grabbing a coat, I made it through the floors, inspecting every area, and ran to catch the train. I did feel a little odd as it made its way to Effingham Junction, and changed trains to the next station on a separate line—Cobham. I even made the walk to 28 D'Abernon Drive. But I didn't survive the evening. I was in bed in no time at all and woke on Christmas Day to a somewhat bewildered, offended mother. But it was the only time they were ever to see me with too much drink in me.

If *Yes Minister* was true to life in Downing Street, *Are You Being Served?* was a close runner-up when it comes to departmental store life. Perhaps it is the repetitive ordinariness which causes the unusual to appear so hilarious. At one stock-taking session, I was asked to work on a Sunday. With the store closed we reckoned more would be achieved. I was asked to check sheets of stock—three on a page—to make sure that those who had put the inventory together had done their work properly. I was assigned to the head of Electrical Goods, Mr Fowler. 'Fowler by name, foul by nature,' staff joked.

The work virtually completed, I questioned why one sheet had not been covered.

'Oh, that's in the old lift-shaft engine room,' Mr Fowler dismissed quickly. 'When they took the old lift out they put in a new lift elsewhere and made the old engine room into a storeroom for my stock—you don't want to see that.'

But I took this job seriously. 'I'm afraid I do,' I insisted. We climbed onto the top floor, familiar steps which also led to the display studio. We walked along the corridor to the old lift-shaft. Quite what happened still isn't clear, but somehow I touched a fire-extinguisher gun on the old lift-shaft door, which promptly went off and exploded on Mr Fowler!

To this day I cannot work out how so much white powder can be contained in a small tube a mere one and a half inches by eight inches. Fowler was covered head to toe, with his tie, shirt and jacket lapels being completely covered in white powder, along with his face and glasses. With his index fingers, he wiped away the dust from his spectacles and swore at me profusely. If it is true that the secret link between aspiration and achievement is development, I reckoned my developing skills were about to be cut short. But Mr Fowler suddenly realised that this was acid powder and could eat his clothes away. He disappeared off home in a puff.

One day, the General Manager was looking for the Carpet Manager, whom my team and I had rolled up in a 12' × 9' Indian carpet and stacked up in the corner! The GM never did find out what had happened.

There was also the never-to-be forgotten occasion when I built a Christmas grotto of wire mesh and tissue-paper, which was then spray-painted. It was infinitely better than anything Harrods could have accomplished, in my humble estimation. Having connected most of the lights, I left a few wires bare, deciding to give these attention before the store opened the following morning. Alas, snow fell overnight, trains were cancelled and while I was waiting at Effingham Junction, Derek Horwood my boss, filled with admiration for the fine work, turned on the Christmas lights. He was hit by the most massive shock of electricity hurling him into the grotto!

Sometimes bored, we would stand motionless in one of the major windows of the store for as long as we could, before passers-by realised we were human after all. Occasionally, as people stood looking at the merchandise, one of the display team would give the customer a wink and then revert to the motionless stance.

Eventually, Mr Jeffries, the boys' club leader, moved to Plumstead to care for his elderly sister. Peter Comber— the obvious choice—took over the leadership of the group. Bryan Price and I were sort of second-in-command. The club was altered somewhat with the change of leadership, numbers grew and the annual camps continued. I even began to help 'friar', who cooked for the lads.

But despite a stable family life and fulfilling career, I was strangely unsettled. It wasn't that I needed to leave home, nor could I see myself leading an Oxford–Regent Street display team, or forming my own freelance company. I was yet to learn that self-disillusionment is necessary for spiritual maturity. But instead of seeing disillusionment as a friend, I viewed it as an enemy. It was on these rare and infrequent occasions that depression turned to darkness and I took excursions into the pleasures of sex with friends. It certainly relieved the tension, but afterwards I felt even deeper guilt and shame. To me they were excursions into a betrayal of important moral values. I knew I was spoiling other lives as well as my own.

It was playwright Jonathan Miller who, on a national television broadcast, stated categorically that the 'orifice' into which one puts one's 'private parts' was unimportant—and has nothing to do with morality. AIDS was not yet discovered, but I knew he was wrong.

May 12th, 1962 was a fine spring day. At around 8 pm

that Saturday evening, two friends, Geoff and Colin, met on the pavement outside our house. Parked nearby was a 125cc motor-bike belonging to Miriam's boyfriend.

'Can you ride this?' one asked.

'Of course,' I replied, not wanting to look a fool. I'd never been on a motor-bike in all of my life! In moments, I was astride the machine and was being pushed down D'Abernon Drive, as the bike was minus a kick-start. The cool evening breeze refreshed me despite depression, as I passed the home of a racing-driver who had recently been killed in a circuit crash.

As I neared the apex of the oval-shaped road, I negotiated cars that were parked, staggered on either side of the road. D'Abernon Drive was only wide enough for two cars to pass each other. Most houses had a car or two, but not many were built with garages. If all the cars had been parked on one side of the road only, it would have made the whole circuit impassable, so cars were staggered all the way round the road on each side. I wove in and out of the cars with great success.

The last thing I remembered was glancing over my shoulder, proud of this new-found motoring success. The road turned to the left, but with the twists and turns, I was unaware that the front tyre had burst and the wheel was about to clip the kerb. As it did, I shot over the handlebars like a rocket and hit my head on a large brick pillar, one of two holding up wrought-iron gates.

One hundred metres away, unaware of the impending accident, Geoff and Colin commented to Dad, 'Well, Mr Coates, we've got a right little Stirling Moss here!'

Dad wasn't impressed. 'I'll Stirling Moss him when he gets back.'

I didn't come back—not for many weeks. Upon impact, I split my head open, blinded my left eye and fractured almost every single bone in my body. The bloody, crumpled heap lay in one place, while the roaring engine of the bike continued fifty feet away. Intuitively, Dad began the short sprint from the house to the scene of the accident. He rounded the corner to see me lying motionless on a blood-soaked pavement.

Without thinking, he picked me up in his arms, unaware of the serious injuries and broken bones. Carrying me back to 'Mirald' (the name of the house, a mixture of Miriam and Gerald), he laid me on the sofa, and in a state of shock reached for the phone and dialled 999.

'Gerald!' shouted Mum, still in the kitchen and totally unaware of what was happening, 'Stop that stupid noise!' I didn't. I couldn't. Unconscious on the sofa, I was gasping for air as blood poured into my nose and mouth. 'I shan't say it again—stop that noise!' she shouted, striding into the living-room in a menacing fashion. According to Dad, she remained vertical for about three seconds, took in the sight of her son on the sofa saturated in blood, and fainted.

The only emergency vehicle available at the time was a St John's ambulance. Within sixty seconds of answering Dad's call, it was alerted to another emergency crisis. 'If we had responded to that call sixty seconds before your own,' the ambulance driver, Syd, told Dad, 'your son would never have lived.'

Mum and Dad followed the ambulance as it left Stoke D'Abernon with siren wailing. Police manned the traffic-lights in Esher and gave them a police escort to Kingston Hospital. Mum and Dad lost them in minutes. By the time they arrived at the hospital, it was almost 8 pm. They were told, 'Your son has about four hours to live. You may as well go home. He'll never regain consciousness. We'll call you at midnight.' For the next seven days, I didn't regain consciousness. During the seven after that, I remained semi-conscious.

Transferred to Atkinson Morley Hospital in Wimbledon (then one of Europe's top brain-hospitals), I was given electric shock treatment to determine the brain damage. I had already undergone an operation, had experienced the pain of a lumbar puncture and the hair on my head had been shaved of with a cut-throat razor. The noise of an electric shaver, it was feared, could do further damage. The brain-tests were negative. But the first shock didn't take and nor did the second! Before getting the results they were looking for, I passed out—with shock! My parents were now told: 'He is likely to be in hospital for three months and a convalescent home for six.' They were grateful.

'It will be nice to have him home for Christmas,' Mum told Dad.

In the event, I was home not in nine months but nine weeks! Three weeks after that, I was cooking for over 100 boys at the summer camp I had attended for the last five years. Wylie McIsock, my surgeon/consultant, plus the nursing staff, had been marvellous. They called me their 'miracle boy' and couldn't explain the remarkable recovery.

A right little Stirling Moss? Stirling had been involved in a major accident himself. He was in the same hospital, virtually opposite me. It was to be the end of Stirling Moss's career as the top racing-driver. But this experience was to be the beginning of something new for the aspirations that had eluded me for so long. The five clots of blood surrounding my brain dissolved. Sight was restored to my left eye and my body healed in a remarkable way. Hair was growing back again. The prayers of my friends were being answered.

It has been said that death (or nearness to it) concentrates the mind wonderfully. It certainly did in this case. Parents who supposedly didn't believe in God began to pray while I was in hospital. H. L. Reid & Co kept the job open. My best friend and neighbour, Bryan Price, had experienced a crisis of his own. He had slipped into a more worldly approach to life and his attendance at the boys' club dropped off. Saturday was spent cricketing, and compared to his shining neighbour, he looked a reprobate. He was probably being more honest than his schizophrenic friend in hospital.

He was told of the accident at the close of the day's play, put down his pint, walked home, went up to his bedroom and surrendered his life to Christ. 'It should have been me not him,' he said.

I knew what I had to do once home from summer camp. I decided to join the Gospel Hall which had been attended by Mr Jeffries. Bryan Price joined me. I had been along on a few occasions, encouraged by Peter Comber, and knew a few of the folk there. They had all been praying for me.

The very first Sunday I went along, I was warmly welcomed. I was to be there for the next six years. Sunday evenings were a fairly cheerful mixture of good hymns and speakers. At 6.30 pm sharp, the meeting started and usually at 7.30 pm sharp, it finished. A young evangelist made a great impression; he was clear, concise and extremely funny. His name was Doug Barnett. There were others who came those Sunday evenings who were to influence me and help model the Christian faith. I have long since forgotten their names, but God has his own method of recording people's usefulness to others even when they are unaware of it themselves.

The news was announced that a missionary from Portugal was to visit, and there had been no small fuss made about this particular engagement. I had a vivid imagination, but was quite unprepared for the shock of seeing an extremely unimpressive, skinny, rather large-eared individual appear. He wasn't the sort of person I was normally attracted to. But I felt he ought to speak at the youth group (a mere seventeen or eighteen people) which I was helping to lead.

On the way out, the missionary put his arm on my shoulder as we stood on the steps of the Gospel Hall and uttered words I've never forgotten: 'God is going to use you in a very special way, young man—I just know it.' Did he know something I didn't know? Later I wondered whether or not the missionary was 'charismatic'. The church was opposed to anything remotely Pentecostal or charismatic.

Occasionally, Mr Rufus Levitt, Mr Jim Smyth, Mr Howard Fellowes, Mr Frank Smith, Mr Arnold Amess and younger men, including Peter Purchase and Rex Maffey, all members of the Gospel Hall, would speak. They were good people and helped the dynamic duo from Stoke D'Abernon in those important years. Then we attended the mid-week prayer meeting and Bible study, which, on reflection, was a fairly dreary half-hour of prayer from the same people, praying the same things. But their sincerity was never in question. The Bible studies from Rufus Levitt and Howard Fellowes, as well as Mr Paget and Mr Rodgers from nearby Brethren assemblies, exposed us to excellent teaching, and a good understanding of the ways of God.

On occasion, there were questions and answers. I liked those sessions. We had gone through a book in the Bible, 1 Corinthians, week by week. Spiritual gifts of tongues, prophecy and healing had been ignored. In the question time, I was keen to understand as much as I could, so I asked, 'Why don't we speak in tongues today?' It was a purely academic question. Virtually any answer would have satisfied me, green and uninitiated as I was.

There were muffled grunts and antagonistic comments. 'These young people are never satisfied,' was

heard coming from the back of the hall. It was to be
several years before I realised the significance of my
question and their response. I was told, politely, by the
man leading the study that tongues was before the Bible
was completed, as a gift for the immature, and was not
needed today as we now have the whole Bible. I was
quite happy with the answer and wasn't quite sure what
the fuss was at the back of the hall. But I was to find out.

These people at the Gospel Hall understood me, or so I
thought. Tea on Sundays at the homes of the Purchases
and the Amesses, as well as at the bungalows of Don and
Joan Everett and Mr and Mrs Smith was appreciated.
Sometimes there would be an 'after meeting' and light
supper: I enjoyed the socialising.

It was now time to be baptised. It was Mr Amess who
baptised me. He was a forester by trade, and was later to
be responsible for looking after Claremont Park in
nearby Esher, once the garden of Claremont House,
built for Lord Clive of India. Friends and relatives were
invited to the baptism, but only a few came. The
floorboards were taken up to expose a tiled baptistry
four feet deep, which was partly filled with water.
During the meeting, along with others, I was fully
immersed in the water and later I was given a card with
the words: '"The Lord shall guide thee continually and
satisfy thy soul." Isaiah LVII XI.'

On the inside of the card was a picture of the baptism
of Christ in the Jordan, reproduced from the original
oil-painting by E. Goodwin Lewis. Mr Amess wrote
'Lord's Day July 25th, 1965'.

Although Mr Amess was at times a distant character, I
appreciated his common sense and open home. His wife
was a marvellous cook and given to wonderful hospitality.
Within a short while, we were to part company—but not
yet.

Jim Smyth worked for an organisation called Counties Evangelism, based in Pyrford, Surrey. Jim came from a straight and somewhat narrow Brethren background, and travelled the country evangelising. He was a typical evangelist, gregarious, passionate and inspiring. Again like most evangelists, he only had one message—the gospel. He would often recite:

> To lose one's wealth is much,
> To lose one's health is more;
> To lose one's soul is such a loss
> That nothing can restore.

He impressed on me the importance of not losing mine! But sometimes it seemed difficult.

Back in Epsom, coffee, lunch and tea breaks with staff were a welcome oasis amidst the frenetic activity that surrounded us. During one coffee break, a girl asked me the time. She worked on the fashion floor; her name was Anona. She lived in Effingham with her parents and younger brother. She had recently left school, and was just fifteen—three years my junior.

One day, I received a message through a third party letting me know that Anona liked me. I was flattered; I liked the company of girls, but wasn't sure I wanted to get matched to one yet. She was a church-goer.

The other women on the fashion floor bullied me no end. I retorted, 'Just because she's gone to church, it doesn't mean she's a Christian any more than being born in a garage makes you a car!' I'd picked that up from somewhere or other, though it never seemed to satisfy Anona's workmates. So I hit on an idea. I would take her to *The Sound of Music* at the West End in London. The story was based on Christian principles, so I thought this might influence Anona. I also prayed for her.

Anona was obviously keen to meet again and so was I.

She often felt depressed, mainly because of conflicts with her father who was very strict and difficult to please. Her mother tried hard to keep the peace. With a younger son, an aged parent and lots of animals to look after, her mother had her hands full.

Anona was not free to invite friends home. So 'going out with Gerry' for quite a while meant just that. She took to my parents straight away and was very much at home in a house full of teenagers. She would usually stay at our house over the weekend.

Not long after *The Sound of Music* stage show, an evangelistic mission led by Jim Smyth took place in Cobham Recreation Ground. Although it was well attended by members of the various Gospel Halls in the area, very few visitors or outsiders came along. Teenagers looking for something different did occasionally make a visit and Jim handled them very well, both publicly and privately. I took Anona along. Night after night, she was subjected—though not against her will—to talks which were obviously aimed at her. One night we both went and spoke to Jim in his caravan, parked next-door to the marquee. Anona prayed a prayer of repentance and commitment to Christ.

Later she confessed, 'I really don't know if I came to know the Lord that night or not. There was so much pressure around, but I did admire the courage and sincerity of both Jim and Gerry.' It was several weeks later, without that pressure, that she asked for God's forgiveness for the past, cleansing for the present and the gift of the Holy Spirit for her future.

The two of us went to the Gospel Hall almost every Sunday and Thursday evening with Bryan and his girlfriend Jennifer. She lived in Morden, so they alternated between Cobham and Morden. Bryan and I volunteered to be on a cleaning rota. For two or three years, we polished the floor, dusted the chairs, cleaned the windows and, with a team of others, kept the place spotless.

In 1966, Billy Graham came to England. Earl's Court was the venue for an average of 27,000 a night to hear his message for almost a month. Although the people in the Gospel Hall had little to do with other Christians, they did go to the Billy Graham meetings. We had never seen anything like it. It was obvious that one could be a Christian and not be part of the Brethren or attend a Gospel Hall. A new flame stirred within us both.

After my baptism, we were encouraged to attend the Sunday morning meetings, which consisted of an hour without anything other than a Bible, a song book, and bread and wine. There was no leader, no music or instruments, and each person present was free to get up and pray, speak, bring a scripture or announce a hymn. Well—not quite everybody. The privilege was only open to men. Women did lead the Sunday School, and had an excellent women's group, but were not allowed to speak publicly or pray when men were present. Soon Anona was baptised, and her parents and friends didn't come either. From then on, Anona would often stay for weekends at my home, and I began to visit her home in Woodlands Road, Effingham. Her grand-mother had died.

But this growing flame was to be the eventual cause of a break with tradition and the Brethren. The first major crack took place on a Sunday morning. Most mornings were predictable. We prided ourselves on not having a set order of service 'like the Anglicans', but in fact we were no less set—it just wasn't written down! A very small selection of hymns was all that was ever sung. A few scriptures centering around Calvary or the sharing of bread and wine with Jesus and his disciples were read. The prayers fitted in with that. There tended to be no more than five or six 'themes' in a year. We felt we were being 'led by the Spirit' and, in so far as we were aware of his activity, we probably were.

It was the bit at the end of Sunday mornings the two of us liked. That was when everybody stayed behind and chatted. Why on earth they didn't serve coffee I couldn't work out. If the first part seemed a somewhat predictable performance, the latter enjoyed a touch of reality, spontaneity, warmth and laughter. Meetings were performance-orientated; there was so much pretence. But I was just about to be caught out, as often I would be—being myself.

One morning, the meeting finished with a hymn, and in the friendly atmosphere afterwards, I walked over to the table situated in the centre of the hall. Chairs surrounded it on all four sides. A broken, half-eaten loaf and a silver goblet half-full of ecclesiastical beverage remained. We had missed breakfast, as we did on most Sunday mornings, when, since there were no buses running between Stoke and Cobham, we walked the two and a half miles. I was hungry. For as long as we could remember, almost each week without fail, one of the senior men recited:

> Only bread and only wine,
> Yet to faith the solemn sign
> Of the heavenly and divine

Put simply, the sacred piece of doggerel declared that those about to share this bread and wine were not Roman Catholics. We did not believe in transubstantiation. That is, the bread and wine did not change in substance. Bread it was, and bread it would always be. I was about to make the mistake of believing what my leaders said they believed.

Without a second thought, I broke off a piece of the white, crusty bread and began to eat it. It didn't seem to be remotely sacrilegious. We were at great pains fifty-two weeks a year to explain this was only bread. Suddenly, the tepid atmosphere turned to a hot house!

'Doesn't your mother feed you?' a somewhat shrill voice shrieked. With a mouth full of bread, I, the aspiring Protestant, looked around to find I was just about the only person left; most were now on their way out of the door.

Embarrassed and somewhat shocked, I reacted: 'This is just bread and wine!' But I was not to get away with it.

'In here, it is the Lord's Supper!' The owner of the shrill voice was behaving like a vest in a washing machine. Not believing my ears, and with the bread still in my mouth, I defended myself.

'But Mr West, the caretaker, makes bread pudding out of this when he gets it home!' The temperature rose swiftly.

'I don't care what Mr West does with it after it leaves here, but while it is in here, it is the Lord's Supper!'

They don't believe this is just bread and wine at all, I thought to myself. They believe in Roman Catholic transubstantiation. What else do they teach and not really believe? I began to wonder whether doubt could be a God-given gift that enables one to come to a knowledge of the truth.

But despite questioning their theology, I had great faith in my leaders. I noticed that nobody in the Brethren assembly smoked cigarettes, or indeed cigars for that matter. Sir Walter Raleigh had not brought the stuff back to the shores of England until after the Bible was written. Had the Bible got anything to say about smoking, and if it hadn't, why didn't anybody smoke? I plucked up courage to ask Mr Smith, who had become a sort of distant father-figure.

'Well, Gerald, the Bible doesn't actually say anything about smoking, for the reasons you've just given. But there is a verse of a hymn we sing which might be helpful:

> Let no earthly cloud arise
> To hide you from your brethren's eyes

I had not learned that hymns and songs are a bad place to get one's theology, but it kept me happy. I am still not sure whether he was serious or not. But within a short while, there was one almighty row when it was rumoured that one of the elders had been seen in the Tartar pub, having a drink and smoking a cigar—after the Lord's Supper on a Sunday morning. But nobody was ever confronted with anything. Things were put under the carpet. When the protrusions wore through, you just laid another carpet over the top of it. People had developed a unique ability to step over and around issues, even if it did make walking difficult.

In the play *In Conversation*, it is said, 'The English have a miraculous power of turning wine into water.' The wine of romance took Anona and me, with Jennifer and Bryan, to a guest-house holiday in Broadstairs. It was a 'proper' affair, with nothing much more involved than a late-night kiss. One windy evening, in a wooden shelter near the beach, Anona had another little prayer answered. I proposed. We became engaged to be married.

On our return to Effingham I, now the aspiring husband, asked Anona's father for permission to marry.

'Well, you've made your bed,' he replied, 'now you must lie in it.' I intended to.

Rings were purchased and exchanged. Life at Epsom, Cobham, Effingham and the Gospel Hall remained unaltered. Anona did make a move to a shop on the other side of Epsom—for higher wages. But that was all.

But the dictum 'Constant change is here to stay' was to mark our lives for a long time yet. It was late summer of 1966. Billy Graham had been to Earl's Court in July. Cliff Richard told the 27,000 present and the press, 'I have given my life to Jesus Christ.' Thousands more were converted to Christ. Shortly afterwards, the small group of young people from the Gospel Hall went on a group holiday. It was a good time and a lot of fun. On our return, we found that the forty souls who gathered at the Gospel Hall had diminished to a little over twenty. 'Should I review my theology on a secret partial rapture?' I remarked, somewhat flippantly.

It was more serious than that. The Plymouth Brethren do not have a pastor or a vicar. Later I would often say, 'Always watch the elder who keeps saying, "We don't have pastors; we don't believe in them"—he is the pastor!' In Cobham there were two men who wanted to run the show. Unresolvable issues surfaced while our group were on holiday—issues we were never to discover. Almost half the little congregation left. The 'stay-inners' were less than gracious to the 'come-outers'! The come-outers were much more gracious to the stay-inners!

Being much more drawn to grace than to hostility, Anona and I missed a couple of Sundays at the Gospel Hall and it was assumed we had left. In the event, that's what we did. 1967 was to be an eventful year. There were now two Brethren assemblies in Cobham, with around twenty members in each. However, the assemblies rely on outside speakers for the Sunday evening and mid-week Bible studies, as they do not have a full-time leader. The Brethren assemblies would not supply our break-away group with speakers, so we had to draw on other evangelical Christians from churches in the area. It was a breath of fresh air.

The new work grew over the next three years, meeting in the Cobham Youth Centre, which was formerly Ebenezer Chapel. It was not unusual for more than fifty people to meet for worship and teaching, and the young people's group we led was a major feature of this growth. But it was not to last, although we were not to know that. We were occupied with other things. Our jobs were demanding, the youth group was growing, and so was the church. Plans were underway to get married. It was a busy time.

The marriage was eventually set for March 18th, 1967; I was twenty-two and Anona, nineteen. For parental reasons, and perhaps partly for traditional ones, we looked for a place to be married near Anona's home. Cobham Gospel Hall was no longer an option. 'It's traditional to be married in the wife's locality,' we were told. But it was understood that we were now 'chapel' as against 'church', so there weren't too many problems with the compromise. We would be married at Cannon Court Evangelical Church in Fetcham—just a short way from my primary school. A leader called Evan Evans was to marry us. Both sets of parents invited an assortment of relatives. Mr and Mrs Evans helped us choose the music, hymns and the order of service, but left the final decisions to us.

Mr Evans' talk at the wedding centred around Mary, Martha and Lazarus opening their home to Jesus and the disciples.

'Your home is going to be used in a special way for the Lord,' he told us.

He could not have known! Evan was Free Church, as opposed to state or historic church. He was vehemently opposed to the charismatic or Pentecostal dimension in worship and church life. We became a source of concern to him within a short while, though we hardly ever met again. But Evan did a great job, and we left for our honeymoon—a boat on the Thames.

We wanted to live in Cobham. But it was one of the most expensive places for property in the United Kingdom. We had heard of a small terraced property in Tartar Road. It was empty, available and for rent. We had no savings. Having contacted the owners, we looked over the house and like any couple with no resources, wanted to get into it as soon as possible. Unexplained red tape and remarkable delays at the property company continued throughout the honeymoon. Parents had told us to look elsewhere.

'Why do you think you're so special? Why do you think God's going to look after you?' Anona's father rebuked her. This would be a test of our faith.

My father collected us when we returned. Hardly were we in the car when he turned and told us, 'We've got some bad news for you.' It was the house. 'It's no longer available.' Faith operates best with the impossible. So until our prayers were answered, we took lodgings in Guildford. When money ran out, we went and stayed with my mum and dad. But the pressure was on!

We didn't want to presume upon Mum and Dad's generosity, and neither did we want to appear to be irresponsible. An advert in the local press advertised what turned out to be a beautiful mews flat in Leatherhead. But we didn't want to live in Leatherhead. Somehow, we sensed it wasn't right. But two married couples in the same property created its own tensions. Agreeing to live in Leatherhead, we arranged to sign the contract the following day after work.

As I was about to leave the studio, the phone rang. I nearly didn't go back to answer it, because I had a train to catch and an agreement to sign. The future happiness of my wife depended on it, but I did return.

'Hello, is that Mr Coates?' It was the property company who owned the house in Tartar Road. 'Do you still want the house?'

Taken aback and somewhat bewildered, I replied, 'Yes.' Bothered I might miss the train to Leatherhead, I paused.

'Would you come to the office tomorrow and collect the keys please? You can sign the papers—the house is yours!'

The journey back to Cobham was exhilarating—I nearly exploded with excitement. Anona and my family were overjoyed. We phoned the kind people at Leatherhead who had shown us round their property, explained the situation and began to make plans to move into Tartar Road.

Because I had been with H. L. Reid for seven years, the management allowed us to buy furniture and flooring at cost. The property had no central heating, of course: not many did then, and we couldn't afford carpets—but it was to be home for the next nine years.

Aspirations had been turned into achievements. I was now married, had a rented home, was a Display Manager and the youth leader of Ebenezer Chapel. The Christian Archery Movement youth leader, Peter Comber, had moved to the Isle of Wight. After leading it for a while we closed the CAM down. We endeavoured to integrate the young people into the youth group. The wine hadn't turned to water. Opportunities continued at all levels. However, I was just about to find out that opportunity is matched by opposition.

We often prayed for Cobham. But little seemed to happen. Few were converted: the town was virtually untouched by the word and the Spirit of God. But the folk at Ebenezer Chapel were most sincere. I wondered if it were possible that in part they were sincerely wrong? The thought was unthinkable. They had done so much for Anona and me!

The flame, though already quite bright, was about to become a fire—fanned by the winds of opposition.

'Jesus overcomes the world by being overcome; Caesar's triumphs chart the way to his empire's decline and fall.'

Malcolm Muggeridge

'Let us run with perseverance the race that is set before us, looking to Jesus, the pioneer and perfecter of our faith.'

Hebrews 12:1–2 RSV

Chapter 4

The Pioneer (1967–1972)

Our new home was used for the youth group, often till late in the night counselling and praying. Ebenezer Chapel benefited from this influx of young people, and we continued to enjoy the new freedom that the elders Mr West, Mr Fellowes and Mr Amess gave us.

The Intelligent Fire had touched my life when I was eleven. Despite the flickering flame throughout those teenage years, it became a small fire after my near-death motor accident. Meeting Anona and helping her come to Christ caused the flame to become stronger. I no longer felt alone. But like many Christians in those days, we were still extremely parochial. Outside of what we read in newspapers and saw at Billy Graham Earl's Court meetings, our lives were locked up to Cobham. Our new church was aptly named Ebenezer Chapel, which refers to the 'Stone of help' where the prophet Samuel said (in AV language) 'Hitherto hath the Lord helped us.'

We had still not met any Pentecostals and the charismatic movement was not underway as far as we knew, but the flame led us on beyond our experience into new areas. While truth can be a gateway that leads us to the

Spirit, sacred ancient writings had told us that normally the Spirit leads us to the truth. We needed more of the Spirit.

An American group, the Forerunners, attached to Campus Crusade for Christ, were in England. The *Evening Standard* had done a feature on their work. Feeling I was somewhat of a young pioneer, I contacted them and they came to Cobham. The Forerunners taught us 'the four spiritual laws' of salvation, including being filled with the Holy Spirit. This opened us to different ways of thinking—but still no gift of tongues, no heavenly language.

One Sunday evening a Miss Elsie Kidd, a diminutive lady of Indian origin, gained my attention. I had already run a successful month-long series of evangelistic youth meetings in a coffee-bar atmosphere at Cobham's village hall. It was called Tempo. It was something of a dump even then. Demolished at the close of 1989 to make way for a brand-new, architect-designed block of shops, offices and homes, its then-dismal features were masked by low lighting and coloured spotlights. Scores of teenagers had come in from the area, several had become Christians, and some joined the chapel. Converts were 'followed-up' and special teaching sessions were arranged.

It was at one of these that Miss Kidd appeared. 'I have been praying for this area for thirty years,' she whispered. 'I know you're the answer to my prayers.' I was astounded. This happened in books, in other countries, but not in real life in a place like Cobham! Her prayer was for a new sort of church to emerge, something that would be true to Jesus and to Scripture, something that would be effective. She talked much of candlesticks and candles, flames and fires. I hardly had a clue what she was talking about. But the inner flame responded.

When Elsie died several years later, she was probably

concerned at the way her candlesticks were shaping up, and the direction of the flames! But I often thought, 'How good it would be if she had been around now, and could see just how intelligent this flame that God has given us really is.' Perhaps the Great Bookkeeper was keeping a record of all of this, and she could read about it in the age to come.

Apart from Miss Kidd's comments, she was to take one further step that would seal our direction as pioneers. She had a friend, who lived in Chelwood Gate across the road from one-time prime minister Harold MacMillan. She was keen for me, still in my early twenties, to go to a small conference held in the house. She also invited Alan Kay, a colourful figure at Cannon Court Evangelical Church, where, strangely enough, we had been married. I wasn't at all sure what it was all about.

Miss Kidd told us, 'They're waiting on God about the state of the nation.' A man ten years my senior would be there; his name was Roger Forster. I already admired Roger, who had spoken in several home-meetings in Cobham. Had it not been for Roger, I probably wouldn't have gone.

It was a small affair, and I was glad to arrive after a somewhat uncomfortable journey in a van driven by Alan Kay. Alan was influential in his own church in Fetcham; he was something of a pioneer himself, and a multi-gifted handyman. His semi-detached house in nearby Leatherhead was rewired so that from the head-board in his bedroom, he could turn on just about every appliance in the home. It contained over 200 light bulbs, spotlights and appliances. The spotlight was now to be put on me!

'If it's all right with you two, we are going to fast for the next few days,' a somewhat precise man with a military bearing told us as we arrived at the door.

Fast! I thought to myself. I'd hardly missed a meal in

my life! We unpacked and went down to supper.
Strange sort of fast, this, I reckoned. I didn't know
anybody there, and Roger Forster was far too important
to shout across to. We were by far the youngest of the
party, and, other than a few polite comments, no one
spoke to us. I was beginning to wish I hadn't come.

The same man who met us at the door stood to his
feet at the close of the meal. 'Well—let's go on to Zion!'
My mind raced. Where on earth are we going? Where
on earth is Zion? I'd only heard about it in the Psalms.
Zion turned out to be a small house in the grounds of
the main one!

The next few days were dreadful. Songs were sung
which we didn't know, scriptures were read which I
didn't understand, and subjects were discussed upon
which I didn't even have an opinion. End-time truth,
eschatology, the kingdom, the church, yes—and even
Zion! We fasted during the day—but being a lover of
coffee, I spent most of my time nursing a massive
headache. While prayers, discussions and songs were
going on, however, I was working on a plan.

In the centre of the room was a small table, on which
was placed a large bowl of fruit. The spiritual conferees
didn't need any—they could wait for the evening meal. I
was trying to look wonderfully spiritual, but I was also
desperately hungry. The plan involved how I could nip
off to the loo, nick an apple on the way, and munch it
before returning. I failed! My hunger kept the plan
alive for three days. Pride didn't allow me to take any
fruit for fear someone would see what was happening.

Meetings started shortly after dawn and went on,
without a break, until midnight and beyond. The only
time I opened my mouth was when the man with the
deep voice, Maurice Smith, asked about the successful
coffee bar and evangelistic meetings we'd had in Cobham.

Alan Kay was excited. He drove home praising God,

often with his hands in the air! 'What a wonderful conference!' he exclaimed to me. 'Maurice has told me there is going to be another one, and wondered if we'd like to go. I've told him yes!'

I, with a headache, groaned inwardly but, still keeping up the professional front, responded, 'Oh yes—wonderful!'

But the dreadful experience had rocked me, and challenged my faith and understanding of the Scriptures. Soon, I began to read every book I could on the Holy Spirit, from John Stott to David du Plessis. A Christian organisation had opened a bookshop at the end of Cobham High Street. The Moody Blues later purchased it as a centre and record shop. John Lodge, who with Justin Heywood wrote many of the Moody's songs, was to come to faith himself in Detroit. The experience was to have a major bearing on his own view of life.

The headache continued. Not a physical one now, but a theological one. I knew I had the Holy Spirit, so how do you get more of the Holy Spirit? I'd already worked out that it was the work of the Holy Spirit to pay Jesus the highest accolade, and the work of Jesus to pay his Father the highest accolade. I needed the Holy Spirit in a greater measure for my own quality of life, to close the credibility gap between my private thoughts and the public front. I wanted to see God's power when I preached.

Michael Harper, who lived a few miles away in Molesey, had launched an organisation called Fountain Trust which worked for the spiritual renewal of denominations. Speakers at conferences and celebration events included Denis Clark, Campbell McAlpine, Cecil Cousen, Arthur Wallis and Jean Darnall. They were to be influential in the nurturing of the charismatic movement, which spread beyond the denominations—but they were not to know that then.

Visits to such conferences were not encouraged. Neither Alan nor I (who continued with a theological headache) were on any mailing lists. We heard about the meetings by word of mouth. We only went to a few at the Metropolitan Tabernacle in London before it reverted to the kind of Calvinism that refused to host charismatic meetings. Alan Kay had been baptised in the Spirit and was speaking with tongues. I hadn't, and it was an embarrassment.

But I had another theological problem. Clearly, the people that were at the meetings I attended in London loved the Lord Jesus and had experienced the power of the Spirit. But some of them came from churches whose leaders, and particularly vicars, didn't believe in the authority of Scripture, or the power of the Spirit. These leaders were certainly not evangelical, in any sense of the word. The Fountain Trust promoted renewal, and individual lives were renewed. How could entire denominations, often led locally or nationally by what could only be termed unbelievers, become channels for revival?

Is a new sort of church needed? I asked myself. What sort of church should it be? It had to be one which, if Jesus lived in Cobham, he'd be happy to be part of. I was about to learn a vital lesson: having babies is much easier than raising the dead!

Arthur Wallis began to write quite radical literature. I could never work out why someone who wasn't the most exciting speaker on earth should be such an excellent writer!

One day, a special meeting was called by Mr Fellowes, one of Ebenezer's leaders. An excellent Bible teacher, warm and gracious, he'd been very influential in my life; perhaps more than he ever knew.

'Gerald, we have some news for you.' He went on to

explain that it was too much of a pressure having 'two tables' in the same town. He was referring to one of the central points of the Brethren assemblies—the Lord's table. 'We're going back,' he explained.

Negotiations had gone on for quite a while, and Mr Fellowes was aware it was likely his young pioneer would not want to go back into the Plymouth Brethren because of our Pentecostal connections. In real terms, there were no Pentecostal connections. We'd never met a classic Pentecostal from the Elim or the Assemblies of God. I still wasn't speaking in tongues. I had, in fact, only heard tongues once, and that was at the conference at Chelwood Gate. As I didn't know I was in a Pentecostal meeting, I thought a Russian was present and was praying. I imagined the interpretation was simply a prayer.

So that was the end of Ebenezer Chapel. Some returned to the Gospel Hall, and Anona and I were left with three friends, Roger, Penny and Linda. A few people moved away, including a certain Mrs Runciman, whose husband had died several years previously. She had been influential as a mother-figure in our lives, but returned to New Zealand. A few others were somewhat shocked at these events. They were shaken in their faith and, unable to go back to the strictures of the Plymouth Brethren, ended up nowhere.

For the first Sunday or two, we just didn't know what to do. We knew we couldn't go back to the Gospel Hall; the flame was leading in another direction. There was no other evangelical church in the area, and we had no transport to go to the Baptist preaching centres in Guildford and Walton. So the first Sunday or two was spent feeling guilty because we were not going to church. We sat at home and read the Bible, but were troubled about where this growing flame would lead us.

Eventually I decided to gather the five one Sunday

morning. The coffee-table was placed in the centre of
the room, a white table-cloth covered it and a plate was
placed on one side with some bread. Ribena was diluted
in a glass. The atmosphere was not so much religious as
embalmed! I stood in the doorway of the front-room,
which measured 12' by 14'. 'God in heaven—what am I
doing?' I exclaimed out loud!

I'd come out of the Plymouth Brethren, but the
Plymouth Brethren had not come out of me. I'd simply
transferred the Gospel Hall into my front-room. So I
took the cloth off, put the coffee-table back under a
bookshelf in the alcove, and left the bread and the
Ribena on the television. It was a start. Even I knew that
Passover and the breaking of bread was always in the
context of a meal and fellowship—never a competition
as to who could take the smallest nip and sip in empty
silence.

David Taylor, who went to the local Methodist church,
had become a Christian at one of the Billy Graham
meetings. He began to meet with the small group of
five, as I was an old school-friend. Mary Limmer, an
Anglican Christian from nearby East Horsley, also began
to meet with us when Anona started work at the Army
and Navy departmental store in Guildford. One or two
other young people in a local church youth group heard
about these strange goings on at the Coates' household,
41 Tartar Road, and were intrigued. But the meetings
were not public, and we made no attempt to visit other
churches or fish for new members.

There were a few other experiments of a similar
nature going on in the United Kingdom: Halford
House in Richmond, Manor House in Chard, Somerset
and Honour Oak in South East London. Other lights
were emerging—Barney Coombs in Basingstoke, John
Noble in Romford—but they were early days. There

were no networks with magazines, Bible weeks or anything of that nature. As far as the 'fabulous five' in
Cobham were concerned, we were on our own. Maurice
Smith occasionally dropped in, and an impromptu
meeting would be held. He had remarkable charisma,
and his ministry consisted of telling stories with quite
incredible insight. He had what was to be called
revelation—and that was precisely what it was.

One or two of Maurice's friends would drop in as
well, such as John Noble and Ted Crick, often on their
way to other meetings. It was around this time that
Keith Bentson and Orvill Swindoll from Argentina
visited some of these new churches. They were experi-
encing something of a revival. They evangelised, planted
new churches and created leadership structures to oversee and care for the growing numbers being added to
their churches. Although their period of influence was
brief, it should not be underestimated. It was just the
boost we needed.

Dr and Mrs Gilchrist lived in Icklingham Road, the
smarter end of town. They had always taken an interest
in us as a couple even when we were in the Plymouth
Brethren. As a somewhat arrogant young man, I told
Mrs Gilchrist that whenever she went to church, she
ought to wear a hat or she was being unbiblical and
displeasing God. I apologised years later.

The Gilchrists had a friend, Tom Rees, a well-known
evangelist who was going to have a series of meetings at
London's Royal Albert Hall, entitled 'Time for Truth'.
Tom's pianist was a man we would share a home with
for seven years, but as yet we'd never met. The meetings
never happened. But I liked the name.

In the autumn of 1970, a series of meetings, entitled
'Time for Truth', were held at Cobham's village hall—
which had been renovated. On the outside, it still looked
as though it was about to topple over, but the inside

looked a little safer. Despite advertising in other evangelical churches, very few visitors attended. A dozen or
sixteen gathered to hear our friends Smith and Crick. It
was a disappointment. I didn't realise that God does
more behind our backs than in front of our faces. But
a young man from Morden heard about what was
happening. His name was Mick Ray. He attended one
or two of the meetings, brought friends, and when he
married Liz, moved to Cobham. They, along with
others, acted as a core for what was to be an influential
group of Christians in a somewhat inconspicuous town.

Mum and Dad occasionally visited 41 Tartar Road, but
didn't interfere in our marriage or church affairs.

It was Miriam who phoned me in tears. 'Dad's on his
way to hospital,' she sobbed. It was a complete surprise.
Dad had just collected Miriam after a little shopping. He
parked the car in front of the garage. It had been
recently erected in the side plot of the garden. He
enjoyed good health, and was rarely off work sick. As he
walked from the car to the front door, he was seized
with a heart attack. He staggered into the front room
and lay on the couch while an ambulance was called. It
was serious, Mum could see that.

'I'm sorry, dear,' he groaned. They were the last
words he was to speak to anyone. He died on his way to
hospital.

The funeral was a simple affair. But to me, the words
seemed so absurdly meaningless. The numbness caused
by the loss of my father was only matched by the
bewilderment about our 'dearly beloved brother', who
in reality had no faith in God whatever, and while
admiring our faith, was cynical about the church—particularly the Church of England.

I would be asked many times, privately and in public
interviews, 'If you had your time over again—what

would you change?' One thing would be the premature death of my father, and later my mother. I should have liked them to have been able to share in my family life, the occasional Christmas, and in the limited 'success' and 'influence' of their son. It was not to be.

It was clear that I couldn't continue with the job in Epsom, look after Anona (now expecting our first child) and look after this growing fellowship. We were not into meetings and services with a hymn, a prayer and a chat. There was a great deal of friendship, counselling, prayer and getting to know each other—and having no secret areas to our lives. Parents did not understand about this somewhat new group, and young zealots don't always make it easy for parents to obtain that understanding.

The growing group was becoming something of a demand. Edwyn Pelly was the son of a naval commander who had served on the *Ark Royal* battleship. His private education was finished off in New Zealand. He'd committed his life to Christ shortly before the trip out there. Upon his return, he got linked in with this new radical group and was baptised in the Holy Spirit. But Edwyn was a little bit of a sceptic.

When the group went off on holiday to the Lake District, there were lots of jokes about the size of the cereal bowls he ate from each breakfast time. They were enormous. Later, he visited me in my small terraced house and explained that initially he was hurt at the jokes, but realised afterwards something was wrong. 'I have this strange feeling, every time I sit down and have a meal, that I'm never going to eat again.' He piled his plate high, ate and ate and ate—and never put on a pound. He had purchased six of these gigantic cereal bowls, hiding five in a cupboard so that if one broke, he'd have spares.

'This is demonic, Edwyn,' I found myself telling him.

Edwyn wasn't sure if he believed in demons, and he certainly didn't like the idea he might have one. Prayers were prayed in the name of Jesus, and Edwyn involuntarily choked out something quite invisible.

He looked shocked. 'Grief—I've never experienced anything like that!' Edwyn went home and smashed up his other bowls, and from that moment on began to eat normally. He also got rid of the silly, but none the less real fear of never eating again.

Linda was an attractive teenager, but broke down in the worship one evening. Mary Limmer, Anona and I took her to the dining-room and heard, amidst her sobs, that she was full of fear.

'I'm afraid of the devil, ghosts, poltergeists, the dark, walking out alone—I'm even afraid of God, because I can't see him.'

We knew that most people who were afraid needed a jolly good dose of the love of God. There is no fear in love. But this was something different. 'Would you like to be free of this fear?' I asked.

'Oh, yes,' she replied.

Thanking God for Linda, I quietly prayed in the name of Jesus. She screamed, leaped up and, with her fingers stretched out, attempted to gouge my eyes out. I half rose off the chair, and shouted, 'Out—in Jesus' name!' With that, the girl slumped back into her chair, and all the colour came back to her face. But I was shaken and was shaking! Hesitantly, I enquired, 'Are you OK, Linda?'

She replied with a smile, 'Fine, thank you.'

Nervously, I joked, 'You should have seen your face!'

As quick as a flash, she replied, 'You should have seen yours!'

As we thought and prayed about the dilemma of the growing fellowship, I decided to abandon my career.

What would bring me a source of income, but give me lots of time? I would become a postman! I applied for the job, got it straight away, and started one dark, cold, windy morning at 5.30 am.

This continued for almost another two years. I would often get up at 4.30 am and start work at 5 am, sorting out sacks of mail and then 'throwing it up' into the frame. The walking and cycling kept me fit. I got to know people in the town, and the five rounds which were rotated gave me a good working knowledge of residents and their homes. There was a break for breakfast at around 10 am, but I was often asked to stay on and do overtime, getting home about 2 pm. That left afternoons free to do work on talks and see people for counselling and prayer. Every evening was taken up with the growing group, planning meetings and worship and teaching meetings. I was able to visit Christians in the area who were interested in hearing about what we were doing and why.

Several incidents in that two-year period were not to be forgotten easily. Early one morning, at 7.40 am, I was cycling across the Byfleet Road, zigzagging from house to house delivering mail. It was a main road, and I could never work out why they didn't let me deliver down one side of the road and then do the other on the return route. It was a dangerous exercise.

It was pouring with rain. I saw car lights disappear into one of the several dips. It was such a hilly road. Thinking it was two hills away, I waited and turned right across the road. But the car was only one hill away, and by the time I had waited, the car was upon me. The bike was smashed beyond repair. My leg was broken, and my head hit the tarmac, opening up the wounds of the accident several years previously. Only the day before, I had been pestered by an insurance agent in the Post Office and had signed a piece of paper and given him three pounds. Should I have an accident and be off work, I would be compensated! I did and I was. It helped pay the bills.

The other was a healing. Unsightly warts were growing on the back of my hands and between the fingers. 'We can pull them out or burn them out,' the doctors told me. I decided to pray! Full of faith one day, having prayed for their removal, I opened my eyes and expected them all to have dropped out on the floor. They were still very much on my hands. They had been there for several years.

Three weeks after this prayer of faith, they all disappeared. Whether I was motivated by faith or fear was of no importance—the warts had gone. They never returned.

The insurance was welcome, but it didn't pay the bills. Occasionally I worked on Saturdays, from 11 pm through to 6 am on Sunday morning at a petrol station in Cobham. The manager had children who came to what we now called the Cobham Christian Fellowship. He wasn't particularly well-disposed towards us. Perhaps a small turning point was reached when he admitted, over a meal, to his children, 'Well, I don't like him very much—but he's the only bloke whose money in the till adds up to the petrol which has been sold.'

Cycling and walking on warm, sunny days—or windy, dry days—was one thing: sloshing through the rain, slush and snow, or cycling in freezing conditions was another. Small in stature, my uniform could have fitted Goliath! The peaked cap fitted my head, but the peak was ridiculously large and acted as an umbrella. The trousers had to be shortened by Anona and the belt that held them up was virtually strapped around my chest. I often commented that in order to scratch my chest, I had to undo the flies!

One day, cycling through Cobham, I began to sing one of Charles Wesley's hymns:

> Finish then thy new creation;
> Pure and spotless let us be;
> Let us see our whole salvation
> Perfectly secured by thee
> Keyarunda—sadavoostoo!

Heavens above—I thought to myself—that's not in the hymn-book! But I wasn't sure what had happened, as I'd still not experienced tongues for myself. After several months, I invited John Carter, whom I had met at a conference in Alton, to come and pray for me.

'I need to be filled with the Holy Spirit, John,' I explained.

'Are you sure you're not filled with the Spirit already?'

The idea seemed absurd. Suddenly, I remembered what had happened delivering the mail one day. John decided to help the stream become a river. He laid his hands on my head, and immediately a torrent of heavenly language poured out of my mouth in praise, adoration and worship.

I had met a young man by the name of Graham. He was an administrator at Epsom Hospital who for several months travelled on the train with me via Effingham Junction.

I had told Graham, 'I'm leaving Epsom to do something new.'

Graham seemed a little disappointed, as he enjoyed our chat each morning. 'Oh, what are you going to do?'

Graham came from a well-to-do home; his father drove an old Rover, which looked vintage. How could I tell him I was going to become a postman? Pride reared its ugly head yet again. 'Well, I'm going to be a missionary. I'm not sure how it's going to work out yet, but that's what I want to do.' Graham was impressed.

Several months later, the pioneering missionary had delivered mail at a large house in Fairmile Park Road. I was drenched to the skin and barely recognisable under the ridiculous uniform. The mail was wet—something I could be reprimanded for.

As I cycled out of the tarmac drive, a sports car drove up. It was not unusual to be chased up driveways by individuals asking directions to the police station, fire station, or another part of Cobham. I braked, slid off the saddle and stood in the pouring rain as the driver came nearer. As it turned out the occupant didn't need to know the way—it was his girlfriend's home. Neither was he going to stop, and only put his foot on the brake because the postman had stopped. As I peered through the window, the driver hit the electric button—down it came. It was Graham! I went the colour of a pillar-box!

'Gerald?' Graham asked quizzically. 'I thought you were going to be a missionary!' I jumped on my bike, blurted out a few words and all but swore. I was furious. How could God allow this? Here I was, being greatly inconvenienced and being made to look a proper Charlie. I never did meet Graham again.

But the long days gave opportunities to sing—which I loved doing—to pray, to think and to plan. Often I would come home, eat a light lunch and fall asleep with my head on my arms on the dining-room table.

Through a magazine entitled *Buzz*, we heard about another Christian who didn't fit the mould. Most people were born originals, but ended up copies. I didn't like copies. That's why I was drawn to Nigel Goodwin. He lived not far away in Earlsfield, near Wimbledon. Nigel had started the Arts Centre Group in London, to care for artists who were Christians and who often worked Sundays and so couldn't attend church. Cliff Richard was a founder-member. As a result of my friendship with Nigel, we occasionally went along to Arts Centre group suppers in London.

Anona had given birth to our first son, Paul, on November 25th (my birthday!) in 1968. Simon was born on November 29th, 1970. We planned not to have any more children. Meetings at Number 41 were packed to the walls. On occasion, the door was taken off its hinges, and over thirty people filled the small front-room, the hall and all the way up the stairs. It was time to leave the Post Office and become a messenger of a different sort.

Two writers had influenced me. One was A. W. Tozer, to my mind a brilliant writer who was way ahead of his time. Prophets are rarely listened to in their lifetime, but have books written about them and statues erected in memory of them after their death. The other was Watchman Nee, who had been in prison for his faith in China for many years.

Watchman Nee taught that you should never share your needs, particularly financial ones. So I felt it wasn't right to take a wage from the small group, which mainly consisted of single people, and Anona and I lived 'by faith'. Actually, we nearly died by it. There was rent on the house, rates, electricity and gas, and soon, four mouths to feed. But somehow, God always got us through. We couldn't afford a telephone, had no central heating, there were no carpets on the floor and we never took holidays. Clothes for both of us were bought at jumble sales for several years. It was not unusual to have the same food for dinner three or four days in a row. Macaroni cheese may be nourishing, but I began to put it in the same category as the school salads!

One day, a somewhat depressed electricity man stood on the door to inform us that we were about to be cut off due to non-payment of a bill. We'd always tried to pay bills, even if it was at the end of the twenty-eight days of grace. Fortunately, I had just paid it, had the cheque stub, and showed the man. 'God—how I hate this job,' he confided, as he went off to another poor household to cut them off due to non-payment.

There was only one occasion when we had no money in our pockets—no bank account even existed—and no food in the house. As a result, perhaps, of a mixture of pride and the teaching of Watchman Nee, we felt unable to share our needs, despite the fact that other Christians in the fellowship had plenty of food in their houses, money for clothes, went on annual holidays and were able to afford a few luxuries.

It was Friday, and the milkman was due for payment. Anona was in tears in the hallway. 'I don't mind for us, dear, it's the boys,' she cried. We had not one single penny between us, nothing to pay the milk bill with, and the larder and cupboards contained a cruet and a bag of sugar. We heard the steps up the pathway and the jangle of bottles, as empties were taken and full bottles were exchanged. The milkman walked away. Instinctively, Anona opened the door and shouted, 'Don't you want me to pay you?' I thought she had gone mad.

'No,' he replied, 'someone up the road has paid your bill and left you that box of food,' pointing to the step. We looked down, and there was a large cardboard box, filled with eggs, bacon, potatoes, a ham and just about everything that the milk-cart carried. We lifted the box, carried it as though it was a baby, went into the kitchen, put it down, and burst into tears, our arms round each other! I would have to believe for a lot more than a box of food in future.

It was clear, however, that God was not going to be limited by the pride of a young pioneer or the remarkable insights of a Watchman Nee. This new church was to be built on friendship, openness and 'no secrets', and that included the leader's. Christian leaders often live under the illusion that 'rules don't apply to us'. The philosophy seems to be that congregations submit to leaders but leaders don't have to submit to anybody. The leaders give the church their full time, isn't that enough? Church members received correction, leaders are beyond it.

Well, God wasn't going to let me get away with that ridiculous fantasy. One of those who had come from Morden in the very early days was Howard Pearce, who picked up my somewhat subdued tones on the phone one evening. 'What's wrong, Gerald?' he enquired.

I explained that things were 'a bit difficult'.

'What things?' he enquired further. I hummed and hah-ed. 'Come on, Gerald, I thought we hadn't got any secrets.'

So I eventually explained that bills weren't getting paid. I'd started a small self-employed business, screening copper plate with local village scenes backed on to black felt. But it wasn't very profitable and was taking up a great deal of time. 'But I've left it to the Lord,' I added somewhat defensively.

Quick as a flash Howard replied, 'Well, perhaps the Lord has left it with us!'

A meeting was called, and I was asked to share my financial situation. With no regular income, I supplemented the occasional gifts that church members gave us with work at the petrol station and the profit I made on the copper plates. An offering was taken up at the meeting. It paid all the bills. It was Anona's friend Mary who suggested some sort of regular income. The group were young, immature, and had no idea what we should be given. And so they began with ten pounds a week.

Within a year we received a large twenty-five per cent increase. It helped Anona particularly. Alongside the other sources of income, it helped pay the bills, made sure there was food in the house and eventually we were able to afford a telephone.

Slowly, the group formulated its own philosophy in the light of Scripture and its own history. Firstly, we became friends. We had already come to the conclusion that we were going to know one another in the age to come. Friendship led to a commitment not to move away every time a new job was offered. That commitment led to a financial involvement. A couple would meet, court, get engaged and then want to be married. They also wanted to live in Cobham, for that was where their friends and commitments were. But they couldn't afford to. But the group reckoned it was better to help the couple, even if it cost us money, than to keep our money and lose friends.

So on a friendship basis, financial help was given with a no-strings-attached arrangement. There was also a strong community spirit. We were in and out of each other's houses, helping each other not only with the spiritual areas of life, but also on our homes and gardens, and often we would go off on holiday together.

In the short term, this had the effect of creating a strong level of love, openness, trust and respect for one another. In years to come, it would make residents of Cobham, especially those who had lived there for most of their lives, feel that there were two sorts of people in Cobham—those in the Cobham Christian Fellowship and those outside of it. This was not a distinction that the group wanted. We would have to address that. When there was a birthday or Christmas party, only members of the church were usually invited. It created a division that would not help us in our aim of bringing a little bit of heaven to where we lived and worked. Unbelievers felt they were definitely 'outsiders'.

The friendship, love, commitment and financial involvement led the group not only to recognise me as their leader, but also to realise that I had weaknesses. My gifts were perhaps obvious. I could speak rather well, was a good organiser and seemed to care for people. The group was growing, many were being attracted to it—not only needy, marginalised people, but professionals as well. What more could be said?

Well—what more could be said was simple. I may have been a good speaker, but every now and then some of the things I spoke about bore little resemblance to the facts! The trouble with imaginative people is that they believe that whatever they are saying is the truth— because they are the ones saying it! Some of the things I said, both privately and publicly, were what I wanted to believe had happened. Accountability was needed.

A broader leadership team was formed and decisions were made, corporately rather than by the nodding-process, in which I decided and everybody else nodded. In one sense it was never quite like that, but it was clear that we needed a better decision-making process. On one occasion, I went to two leaders, Mick Ray and David Taylor. I explained that I had invitations to speak in five different countries as a result of the unusual work we were doing in Cobham. I fully expected them to rubber-stamp the initiative.

It was Mick Ray who said, 'Well, Gerald, not only do we not want you to respond to any of those invitations, we actually don't want you travelling around the United Kingdom, either. We want you here in Cobham. Your wife needs you, your two sons need you and quite honestly, we need you—and you might need us.'

I walked away from Mick's house in Tartar Road furious. 'What do they know about senior-level leader-ship?' I grumbled angrily. 'How can extra-local ministries submit to local elders? Who do they think they are? Don't they know what I'm called to?' Well—they did know what I was called to, and my submission to their counsel created trust that would stand us in good stead for many years to come.

The group of five that began in 1970 was still small, perhaps no more than fifty or sixty. Growth would be accelerated in a quite spectacular fashion—but the pioneer had a lot of jungle to cut down. We had run out of models: we were having to *be* the model! If anyone had gone this way before, the path was not clear.

The kingdom of God is so unlike the kingdoms humans build. John the Baptist heralded the King and the kingdom. But the kingdom came through Jesus as an isolated incident over here, a localised miracle over there, an answered prayer in this place and a kind deed done in that place. One could justifiably have asked how on earth this was ever going to reach the nations. But, fanned by the Spirit, he who is the Light of the World would be a spreading flame within a few decades. It is possible that even by AD 40 there were Christian believers in England. And all that—in just three years of ministry!

What had happened in Cobham during the last three years seemed just as inconspicuous and almost irrelevant. I would often ask in prayer, 'How do you reach a nation?' My prayers were being answered, but God's answers often come in well disguised packages.

Maurice Smith, John Noble, myself and others began to gather leaders in Langham Place, next to the BBC by John Stott's All Souls Church. They were remarkable times of loud praise, passionate prayers and prophetic ministry. By invitation only, they became so popular they were moved to the Bonnington Hotel in Southampton Row. There was nothing else like it in Britain.

At one of these meetings, a certain Peter Hill turned up. He had lived in England, had been a missionary in

India for several years, and on his return to the United
Kingdom was disturbed by the moral degeneration he
found here. He visited Malcolm Muggeridge and decided
to create an organisation which he thought he would
call AMP (About Moral Pollution).

'No, my dear boy,' Malcolm told him, 'let's not have a
march against something, let's march for something.
What about a Festival of Light?'

In September, 1971, 30,000 swelled Trafalgar Square
and then marched to Hyde Park where another group
of several thousand were waiting for them. Arthur
Blessitt and Larry Norman created the 'One Way' sign
by pointing an index-finger into the air. I stood on the
plinth in the square next to Lord Longford.

'What's the difference between this raised finger in
the air and two open hands in the air?' he enquired.

I did my best to explain, but his lordship looked even
more baffled after the explanation. Malcolm Muggeridge
began his talk with 'Dear fellow light-bearers', and
before he could go any further, tumultuous applause
and shouts filled the square, to the surprise of hundreds
of onlookers.

The Nationwide Festival of Light continued in less
public forums. There were Jesus rallies and area-wide
events. It was a crusade for moral purity in the media
and in private and public life. It was not a house church
initiative, though Peter Hill had found comradeship
and support from these new church leaders. He himself
became a house–church leader and eventually related to
Barney Coombs' network based in Basingstoke. Peter
had become a voice for God. That is what I felt called to
be—a voice for God.

I never thought I'd see such crowds again—but I was
wrong. Fanned by the Spirit, the little flames in Cobham
and elsewhere were linking up and spreading. The
Intelligent Fire was at work in places we'd never even

heard of, in the lives of people we'd never met, and in churches of many persuasions.

It was Hugh Latimer who, as he was being lashed to the stake and the flames were being lit, made a brave and heroic cry to Nicholas Ridley as he also faced the flames: 'Be of good comfort, Master Ridley, and play the man. We shall this day light such a candle by God's grace in England, as I trust shall never be put out.'

We should thank God for the lives and deaths of those who stood for truth. They were captivated by the flame that they received from God. Tangible flames seemed almost unreal compared to the Eternal Flame. Tyndale translated the Bible into English. This had the effect of removing power from the priests, who would no longer be able to make the Bible out to say what they wanted it to say. Six thousand copies were printed. Tyndale had the same flame.

Jesus wasn't asking me or my colleagues to die for him—he was asking us to live for him. And that was to be death by instalments. To claim to speak on behalf of God was not an easy occupation. Signs followed apostles; stones seemed to follow prophets. In England it was fashionable to be nothing and do nothing. If that was so, I didn't want to be English.

'Do not be afraid of greatness; some are born great, some achieve greatness and some have greatness thrust upon 'em.'

William Shakespeare

'A Christianity which does not prove its worth in practice, degenerates into dry scholasticism and idle talk.'

Abraham Kuyper

Chapter 5
The Prophet (1973–1980)

A person invariably finds himself in trouble simply for doing the unexpected. It appeared I would often do the unexpected.

Many Christians live with locked-up minds. They think the expected and do what is predictable. Locked between perfectionism and traditionalism, creativity is never given a chance. With women effectively silenced throughout the Christian community, there has been very little room for intuitive skills. The prophets had also been silenced. There were few tears in pulpits or on platforms. Sundays at many evangelical churches were reduced to someone giving 'a faithful word'. Decoded, that means, 'as dead as a dodo, but you couldn't fault it theologically'.

With women and prophets silenced, the church was like an army fighting with one arm tied behind its back, with an eye patch over one eye, hobbling around on one leg.

As a boy and teenager, I was almost wholly occupied with myself. It was only as I aspired and became something of a pioneer (virtually by accident) that I began to sense God's burdens instead of my own. I

87

sensed a call to be a spokesman for God—a prophet. God's army must march, with both eyes open, both hands fighting and both feet moving in God's direction. But speaking for God is one thing—being a prophet? Well, that's another.

It was at a meeting in Bath that I received my first prophecy. Steve Appel led a growing church based in the city throughout the seventies. 'You will take this gospel of the kingdom to many nations,' he prophesied. The gospel of the kingdom—it was to be a recurring theme.

However, the early seventies were not times to prophesy in the evangelical church. To have said, 'Thus saith the Lord,' or even a modern day, 'This is what the Lord would say to you,' would raise major issues. Is the prophet infallible? Is he putting himself in the place of God?

One leading Calvinistic Reformed minister asked, 'If I accept prophecy, does that mean I have to glue the prophecies to the back of my Bible between the last chapter of Revelation and the maps?' Clearly, there were many people who prophesied in Bible times whose prophecies were not included in Scripture—such as the three daughters of Philip—so such a notion seemed absurd. But God had feelings as well as words. What were these feelings?

It was Emil Brunner who stated most succinctly, 'The first and most important thing we know about God is that we know nothing about him, except what he himself makes known.' Even I knew that real Christianity could not be reduced to a set of rational propositions and moral idealism. The church needed revelation and an anointing.

God had initiated a dialogue with humanity—through his Son and by his Spirit. God's answers to problems were never organisations, mass-movements, or even books and tapes. It is always a person. God opens up a dialogue with the person and that person serves God, to get his will done. Every person has a secret to his or her ministry. The more powerful the ministry, the more powerful the secret. What were those secrets?

To me, the greatest curse of the twentieth century was wanting to be understood. Jesus' philosophy in life seemed to be, 'Let's confuse as many people for as long as we can.' Religious people couldn't work him out; he went to parties, told jokes, changed water into wine and was often the life and soul of the party. Party-goers couldn't work him out; he was down at the synagogue, teaching and preaching from Scripture, praying and living a quality of life quite different from those around him. He was an enigma. I felt I could have no better role model.

My secret for twenty years would be a vision—one of a mere handful I received myself—which consisted of my driving along a stony road in a car. There were many bends in the stony road, as I zigzagged through tall evergreen trees that hemmed me in. Eventually, I came to an open expanse of beautiful bowling-green grass. It was a sunny day and small groups of people dressed in smart black and white outfits sat on the grass having Bible studies. To their dismay, I drove my car across the grass, ruining years of hard work and a pleasant environment.

I had no idea what the interpretation could be. I may have been able to interpret other people's dreams but God made sure I couldn't interpret my own—I would need others. I phoned a friend, Ron Wing, who many years later moved to Petersfield in Hampshire and linked the church into the Pioneer network. Ron could interpret dreams.

'The car you're in represents your current situation,' he told me. 'The long road with its bends and twists is a man-made road. The trees represent men that have hemmed you in to this road. Trees often represent men in Scripture. The bowling-green grass is religion. The Bible says, "All flesh is as grass," but the worst sort of grass is religious grass—it looks so nice. You are being called to drive across it. You will ruin and destroy it. People will not be able to rest in it as they have.' I was not sure I liked this interpretation!

The youth leader of Commercial Road Baptist Church in Guildford (later to become Millmead, led by David Pawson) was at a wedding. So was I. The youth leader was not given to visions. It was still in the early seventies. But he saw me standing in the wedding marquee with a crown of thorns on my head. He spoke of suffering and mocking. I didn't like that vision very much, either.

John Carter was the man I had met at a conference in Alton, Hampshire. It was John I invited to the Tartar Road house for the laying on of hands and the baptism in the Spirit. After John had prayed for me, he prophesied, 'The Lord has given you a destructive message; it will be received with great joy and blessing by some and in great bitterness by those who reject this ministry.'

Being a prophet didn't seem to be a lot of fun.

American evangelist Jean Darnall prophesied that I would 'go over the mountains and the hills as though they don't exist' and would 'experience the valleys of life being filled up'. She added, 'You will go from mountain to mountain by invisible bridges and it will astound those who are watching you.' Things were beginning to sound a little better.

Robert was another friend. He brought music to my life. A singer/songwriter, he opened his somewhat musically conservative friend to a wider appreciation of music. But Robert was emotionally demanding. Resources ran out, and after a while our friendship was under great strain. When Anona and I were unwilling to respond to several demands and pressures, Robert and his wife who had been good friends to us, both left the fellowship. But it was a special friendship, one I never forgot.

'Gran' then died shortly after I returned from a trip to America with Howard Pearce. She hung on for several days in Cobham's cottage hospital. The family believed she was waiting 'for Gerald to come home'. I missed her a lot. But the broken bond of friendship between Robert and me—a friendship which had involved us in ministry, songwriting and limited travel—affected me deeply. Later, Robert left his wife to live with someone else. Life seemed so unfair to me at times.

But God was to use it all to get my attention and my tears. God knows that words aren't enough, and often his prophets would dramatise the word God had given them. Shocking situations are often addressed by shocking people in shocking language or in shocking styles. My pride and control needed to be broken.

I was having to learn that a speaker should pay as much attention to what he is saying as his listeners. The word of God is indeed 'sweet to the mouth' but 'bitter to the stomach' when it is digested. 'Prophecy is not simply to foretell the future,' I would often say. 'There are only two directive prophecies in the whole of the Acts of the Apostles. That's a book that covers at least thirty years. Prophecy is given to develop our character—no matter what happens in the future.' God was shaping what was very unshapely.

I was learning slowly that if the people of God won't face God, then the prophets of God must go in and face him. But God is faced not only in quiet solitude, but also in friendships. At one of our conferences I submitted areas of life and character to my friend and colleague Mick Ray. Mick had written several worship songs.

Mick told me, 'There's no question of your gifting, or of your willingness to learn. If I wasn't convinced of that I wouldn't be with you. But you do put people off. You don't always listen to people. Your prophetic intuition tells you that you can save a lot of time by giving people answers before they've even asked you questions. It may help you, but it doesn't help your friends, or those who need to offload concerns, burdens and problems.' It was like a knife cutting into me. These were things I didn't want to hear.

Eighteen months later, Mick encouraged me, 'You've softened, I'm really glad success hasn't gone to your head. You've matured and become a little warmer. You are closer to us as a leader.' I was grateful. This was what I wanted.

I was now thirty years of age, had been married eight years, and had two sons. We were still in the little terraced house, and had been invited to America by Bill Thompson, a tailor in Savile Row who had brought the Full Gospel Businessmen's Fellowship to the United Kingdom. But I had no particular hankering to travel— my concern was the United Kingdom. As for prophesying, well, there wasn't much of that, it seemed.

Barney Coombs and Mike Pusey were both in Baptist churches. I had spoken on several occasions in their churches in Basingstoke and Farnborough. I was appreciative of their friendship and fatherly concerns. Annual conferences were held at Pilgrim Hall in Sussex, attended by around 100 leaders. It was at one of these that Jean Darnall arrived, with a can of film tucked under her arm. *Come Together* was about to hit Britain. It was written by Jimmy and Carol Owens and hosted by Pat Boone; I could see that this would be a major instrument to bring back reconciliation among Christians.

'Jean, you must do it,' I urged her.

'Well, Gerald, there are a few leaders here who don't seem too happy with the musical, especially that it's American and has Pat Boone in it,' she told me.

'Don't worry about them—God's in this thing. Why don't we meet again after you've spoken to other conferences and shown them the film?'

A few weeks later, we sat by a pond just outside Esher. The musical would be staged in Britain and would be based in Cobham. Cobham Christian Fellowship elder David Taylor would help administrate, and travel with a large choir and group of narrators. Pat Boone would fly across to front the presentation. If the house church movement was the most significant movement in the church in the seventies, the Nationwide Festival of Light and *Come Together* were the two major projects of the decade.

A couple of Americans had moved to Cobham and got involved with the Fellowship. They opened a restaurant, The Homestead. Anona and others involved themselves, some in management, others as waitresses. Their home became the base for the *Come Together* nationwide tour. Anthony Cordle, a friend of Jean Darnall's, did a magnificent job in making sure the tour was properly arranged.

If Jesus was a prophet, a priest and a king, it followed that the church's work and ministry was hinged around being prophetic, priestly and kingly. Prophets bring the word of God, priests reconcile and kings wage war on the enemy. But spiritual warfare was not understood by the house churches. So we lived with the tension between being prophetic and priestly. If prophets bring the word of God it tends to divide, whereas priests reconcile. How were these ministries so beautifully and perfectly blended in one man—Jesus?

Come Together was a prophetic statement about the unity of the body of Christ. Jesus' prayer recorded in

John 17 was to be a recurring theme in house groups and large platforms all over the country.

Well do I remember hosting the first major *Come Together* production of the tour. London's Westminster Central Hall was jammed to capacity. I went to the microphone. 'There are hundreds of people outside trying to get in; if you have seats near you, raise your hand and move along so that any seats left are near the aisles for easy access. Please don't sit on the steps or in the aisles—it's not allowed.'

People took little notice. The building was crammed with over 2,500 people. They sat on the steps and stood at the back of the auditorium. The General Manager told us, 'I've not seen anything like this since the Second World War.'

As the opening bars of *Come Together* were heard, I was walking up to the balcony to see if there was any space for the hundreds outside. I found myself breaking down emotionally, as a fresh unity among God's people was taking place. In the break, Pat Boone went out to the hundreds who'd remained. Pat was gracious, answered questions and prayed with us all.

It was still the mid-seventies. New churches were proliferating and lines of communication remained informal, though a new magazine, *Fullness*, was initiated. Editor Graham Perrins and art directors Nick Butterworth and Mick Inkpen were keen for me to write. It gave me an opportunity of communicating things no other publication would have allowed. Fired by their encouragement, two booklets, *Not Under Law* and *Free From Sin*, were also designed by the Butterworth/Inkpen partnership. I was now learning to be shaped up by criticism, as well as learning when to be prophetic, bringing God's clear word into situations, and when to be priestly with a 'soft answer'. If I had a propensity to do the former, I would need to be shaped further with God's wisdom to perform the latter.

Barney Coombs wrote of *Not Under Law*:

> *Not Under Law* spells fireworks. It may produce temporary confusion, and perhaps hurt some. But it will make a vital contribution to the recovery of God's principles in the church. In this little book quite a number of evangelical sacred cows are not merely touched, but slaughtered.

I was almost slaughtered verbally in the aftermath. Arthur Wallis commented, 'By the time I had read the last page I had been cut to pieces. Gerald fights with the sabre, whereas Hugh Thompson slashes with a rapier. But a cut is a cut!'

Peter Hill, John Noble, George Tarleton, Dave Mansell, Maurice Smith and I were arranging major meetings in London. Praise God Together was held at the Friends' Meeting House when almost a thousand gathered. I spoke on 'Pioneers and Settlers', a talk which was only ever given at that one major meeting. But it was, to me, an important message. A national team would soon be put together and would be called the Pioneer Team.

Then we moved to London's Westminster Central Hall for some All Saints nights. Later, 5,500 people filled the Royal Albert Hall. Malcolm Muggeridge was interviewed. I, the minor prophet, liked the major prophet. Was it the same spirit?

Was this aging, balding, somewhat affected, superannuated journalist reading my mind? What were these deep stirrings? Why was I hanging on every word, being carried along by the very tone of Malcolm Muggeridge's observations and predictions? Later, with Anona, I spent many happy hours in the farmhouse home of Malcolm and Kitty.

By the mid-seventies, my mother, Evelyn, had died. Unwell, she was admitted to hospital to have a lung removed. After a successful operation she convalesced, but had a relapse. She was buried with our father. I still miss her friendship today.

Mum left just a little money which Roy, Miriam and I shared. Along with a few gifts we received, this enabled Anona and me, with Paul, six, and Simon, four, to increase our mortgage. We moved from the small terraced house in Tartar Road to 52 Between Streets— an extension of Cobham High Street. Outwardly it was an unattractive house, with small frontage, but we began to paint and decorate and make it home for the next nine years.

Almost 100 people were now meeting at the local Ralph Bell Hall, and most were committed members. Although still largely disregarded by the religious establishment, our participation in the nationwide Festival of Light and *Come Together*, coupled with the remarkable meetings at the Friends' Meeting House, Westminster Hall and the Royal Albert Hall, had given us a higher profile.

On several occasions in the Royal Albert Hall I would be expected to say something, but felt I had nothing to say. However, when I stood, the Spirit of the Lord came upon me. I often found myself weeping over the state of the church. John Noble would often say, 'Gerald isn't prophetic by what he says, he is prophetic by what he is.' I didn't really understand that then.

'Jesus learned obedience through the things he suffered.' If that was true of him, it must be more so for us. Most of us pray best when we are under pressure, but we all try and escape pressure. God has his own way of discipling us in circumstances beyond our control.

The little group in Leatherhead, cared for by Alan Kay, moved to Cobham. I responded to area-wide invitations for teaching and ministry. Mick Ray, Chris Bull and Dave Taylor took over the leadership of the church. Mike and Jenny Blount became good friends and wonderfully filled a relational hole caused by Robert's absence.

Occasionally, I spoke at Bible colleges, including London Bible College. The invitation came from Tim Brawn, who lived in nearby Horsley. He'd met Anona through the *Come Together* presentations. Tim eventually came to work with the leadership in Cobham, to serve us and share the workload. But Tim was a growth ministry, not a maintenance ministry. He lifted a lot of work from our shoulders. But he created ten times more! Being a charismatic personality, every meeting he spoke at created further interest and requests for more ministry.

Tim eventually took a job and became an extremely successful advertising executive. Years later, he had a hand in the LIFE logo for the Billy Graham mission in 1989. The fact that things hadn't worked out wasn't his fault. I had many things to learn about people's skills and abilities and where they fitted best.

The anti-legalistic prophetic message continued, nurtured by the sales of *Not Under Law* and *Free From Sin*. Grateful for my own deliverance from promiscuity, we also released *Homosexuality and the Christian*, which created piles of mail from Christians struggling with thoughts, feelings and sometimes relationships, with the same sex. We sometimes received thirty or forty letters a week all of which I answered myself. Only a few were related to sexual matters. A secretary was employed. One of the rooms in 52 Between Streets was turned into an office and this relieved pressure.

In dealing with these situations, I knew that there are very few problems that are purely sexual. Confession, friendship, open relationships, self-respect and fulfilment help a great deal in lessening, and at times removing, overt sexual feelings and behaviour. Prayers and love give a person back identity and normality. But all this counselling took a lot of time, as these things often had to be said over and over again.

Despite my public passion and sometimes anger, I have always enjoyed a good laugh. We asked for and were given a double-page spread in *Fullness* magazine, to put some humour in it. It was simply called 'Notice-board'. It contained all sorts of trivia, which was a welcome break amidst the weighty issues contained throughout the magazine. The double-page spread was made to look like a large cork notice-board. Pinned to it were all sorts of pieces of humorous nonsense. One piece reported:

> As a travelling man myself, I sympathise with a certain Mr Eves recently when he stated, 'When you are a member of the travelling public there is nothing worse than getting burnt to death in an hotel room you've paid for!'

Other observations included:

> I've just stumbled on the fact that the song 'There is a River' was written by Ruth Lake!

And:

> *Ripened Grain* magazine, in recommending Arthur Wallis' book *God's Chosen Fast*, stated it was 'a must for hungry Christians'!

Conducting another interview with Malcolm Muggeridge at the Royal Albert Hall on one occasion, I recorded the highlight:

> The most wonderful thing a man can know is what the Bible calls being 'born again'. To be born into a relation-ship with our Lord cannot adequately be described in words. To know God and to love God and to seek the

truth in God is the highest aspiration that has occupied the greatest minds and hearts the world has ever seen.

I was the interviewer and noted in *Fullness* that Malcolm received a massive ovation. I went on to say:

This leads me to believe that it isn't so much what is said but who says it. I've been preaching the importance of rebirth for years, and sometimes I haven't even got expenses—let alone a standing ovation!

Friendship with the vicar of Cobham led me, the minor prophet, and he, the moderate cleric, to lead a series of meetings entitled 'The Family Meet'. Between five and seven hundred gathered for worship, drama and teaching at St Andrew's Church.

The vicar was a charismatic evangelical, leading a church which contained charismatic evangelicals, non-charismatic evangelicals, anti-charismatic evangelicals, traditional believers who weren't evangelicals, agnostics and a few atheists. Depression set in. It became increasingly difficult to talk with him, as he clearly didn't want to be a burden to anybody and pretended that all was well.

All was far from well. He had decided to get out of the Church of England and go and take a job in a Christian organisation. Details weren't worked out as well as they could have been, and the job fell through. One day, he wandered through the vicarage garden, went into his garage, shut the doors, attached a pipe from the exhaust through into his window and took his life.

The same ambulance driver who drove me as a seventeen-year-old motor-cyclist to hospital, on May 12th 1962, was called to the suicide, but it was too late. The vicar never regained consciousness; evangelically, nor did the church. A nice man came as a replacement, but he wasn't sure about the need of a clear-cut gospel message people could respond to. It reverted to type.

It became clearer to me that to sit under a ministry of confusion only causes confusion in the minds of the listeners. To sit under a heretical ministry creates heretics, who may well believe right things privately but are willing to support, finance and prop up churches whose faith is far from orthodox. Salvation is nowhere to be seen.

Back home, the family was growing. In January 1978, Anona gave birth to Jonathan, a difficult birth, but a son we were both glad of. Older ladies in the fellowship told us, 'He'll bring you a lot of happiness, you'll be so glad you had him.' They were right. Upon discovering the pregnancy, Anona explained the situation to the doctor. 'Would you like an abortion?' was his first question. She wasn't sick, we were in a position to afford the child and she wasn't mentally subnormal! Legally, there was no reason to offer her an abortion. We were furious. I waxed eloquent: 'No—tell him we'll keep this one—but he can kill off one of the other two!'

The fellowship was growing and there was a stable leadership. The qualities of friendship, love, commitment, respect for leadership and the training of new leaders was developing at a steady pace. In reality, the relationship between the local Anglican church and the Cobham Christian Fellowship had been between myself and the vicar. When he took his life, there were no other sustainable relationships to further the cause of unity. I often quipped, 'We have this wretched week of unity every January—only because the churches don't want unity the other fifty-one weeks of the year!'

Our first car, a Hillman Minx, given by Doug and Maureen Turton (kind Anglicans!), had died and was reduced to a cube. We were now driving a white Vauxhall Victor. I covered the driving seat with a sheepskin rug, as it was in a bad condition. Anona hated the sight of it. She told me I should complete the act by purchasing a couple of sponge dice and hanging them from the rearview mirror. Perhaps 'Gerald and Anona' should be placed across the front of the windscreen in green and white plastic!

On most other things, our tastes were very similar and by the late seventies and early eighties we were in a position to go out and buy some new clothes. Regular financial support from the Cobham Fellowship, and gifts I received from speaking in churches and conferences, enabled a more normal approach to family life.

Meanwhile, Capel Bible Week, the annual event that drew several thousands together, was losing direction. The week was a blessing but wasn't building anything. It gave some a shot in the arm, but created an army who waited for their annual inoculation. But it was most unsatisfying. The prophetic series Bryn Jones gave on Jesus' birth, life, and death was one of the finest things I'd ever heard.

But there had been growing tensions between the so-called London brothers and those who were with Bryn Jones and Arthur Wallis. Quite what the ingredients to the mix were is still not altogether clear. Certainly *Not Under Law* and *That You May Not Sin* (later reprinted as *Free From Sin*) featured in the heated discussions, as did the morality of one of the 'Fabulous Fourteen', and particularly how we handled it.

I was cleaning my car, parked at the front of the house, when a letter arrived. Although the envelope was addressed to me personally, the letter had been photocopied. It was from Arthur Wallis. It listed eight 'concerns' and suggested that some of the London brothers might be motivated by an ambitious, jealous and worldly spirit. Because of the strains and stresses, it was explained that it would be impossible to work together. Although the London brothers phoned and wrote, the issues were not resolved.

In private conversations and small leadership groups, the London brothers discussed and explained the nature of the letter. A good deal of rejection set in. Bryn and Arthur also had to explain the position to men they were working with. Perhaps a quite unintentional spin-off took place. Churches cancelled copies of *Fullness* magazine—after all, it was the publishing platform of the brothers with whom Arthur and Bryn couldn't work. Friendships virtually ceased overnight.

There were not a few who were somewhat pleased with this outcome. Charges of 'This lot will never last' looked accurate. Cynical comments were made such as, 'Well, if this is the result of a church built on relationships rather than on tradition—I think I'd rather have tradition.'

For three or four years we, the London brothers, had to examine the 'concerns' and our own feelings of hurt and rejection. Sometimes these were reactions in the light of deficiencies we felt existed with the other group. But the bottom line was that we loved each other and cared for the work of God and had fondly hoped reconciliation could take place.

Within two or three years, I, along with a small grouping from London and those with Bryn and Arthur, attended a meeting. It was agreed not to go over old ground; Arthur conceded that either his own perceptions about us had not been accurate or that there had been a mellowing on my part and that of John Noble, and our friends. Although this meeting and its outcome were made known throughout the country, damage had been done. The seeds of doubt had been sown and were bearing fruit.

Later, Terry Virgo, based in Brighton and Tony Morton, in Southampton, though grateful to Bryn for his friendship, advice and ministry, ceased to meet together regularly. They created their own teams, ministries, publications and events. Friendship continued between them.

I saw all this not as a major step backwards, but rather as 'a great split forward'. It left more room for creativity and new relationships. We could no longer be charged with becoming a new denomination.

But there were other changes ahead. Capel Bible Week closed down, as the committee could no longer give it clear direction. Some were denominational and wanted to see the denominations renewed. Others belonged to the new churches and didn't believe that would happen in a month of Sundays! Well, actually, they didn't believe it would happen at all. Bryn Jones took the ingredients of Capel and started the Lakes Bible Week, which later became known as the Dales Bible Week and had much clearer direction, and a solid platform of conviction. Later on, Terry Virgo and his team attracted thousands each year to the Downs Bible Week, held on Plumpton Racecourse near Brighton.

In 1979, Kingdom Life, based in Cobham, was started. A 2,000-seater marquee was erected and a local Scout camp was used as a base for several hundred campers. It was mainly a local affair. Speakers included Jim Hammaan from Seattle, a friendly, genial father-figure whom Bryn had introduced me to. Roger Davin from America, singer/songwriter Dave Bilbrough, and Cliff Richard all took part over the next three or four years.

The drama group at the Cobham Fellowship parodied the church and their leader who, due to nasal problems, often sniffed. Over 2,000 people were packed into the marquee the night Cliff arrived. He was in his fifth week

of 'We don't talk anymore' at number one in the charts.
He sang several gospel songs including:

> When I was up in Canada
> I didn't have much money,
> You know my toes were cold and my clothes had holes,
> And my nose was kinda runny—

Quick as a flash he looked round and joked, 'Just like
Gerald Coates!' I told him that one day I'd get my own
back. Perhaps this is that day!

Despite the fact that many relationships had come to
an apparent end, the flame was still burning—in some
respects brighter than ever. I never did prophesy in
classic Pentecostal language. I began to loathe the 'Thus
saith the Lord' type of prophecy. More often than not
people simply strung scriptures together. 'Can't see why
they just don't stand up and read the Bible,' I'd often say.

If the Bible teacher teaches truth because truth is true
at all times, the prophet has to bring truth that is
particularly relevant to a specific situation.

But the nature of my ministry caused me to be
continually looking towards the horizon. One day, I
received a phone call from Jackie Oliver, married to Ian
who led the Ewell Christian Fellowship in Surrey. She
had a vision. There were to be several, all of which
proved to be authentic and important. She saw that I
was keen to get toward my goal, but that I was sometimes
careless with what was around me. This coincided with a
girl in Sheffield, who also had a proven prophetic
ministry, having a vision of me in a race, keen to get to
the finishing line. I shot off course and fell over head
first. Trip wires had been laid for me. I was going to
have to pay more attention to detail, and what was going
on around me.

I'd heard of Sheila Walsh—of course, most people had.
She was Britain's number one female gospel singer. I'd

only heard her sing once, at the wedding of Martin and Sue Scott in Leicester. Martin was at London Bible College with Sue and moved to Cobham to be with friends. Martin would later lead the Cobham Fellowship.

While speaking in Solihull, at the invitation of Brian Pullinger and Pal Singh, I was asked to do a radio broadcast. During the interview, which was interspersed with records, they did a live link-up with a studio in Belfast. Norman Miller, who had worked for one or two well-known gospel record companies, was arranging a Jessy Dixon tour. The next day, they were to be in Birmingham. I was asked to talk to Norman about the tour, the turn-out, the response, and the differences between Jessy Dixon's music and that of other black gospel singers. With the interview over, the line was left open and while the next record played Norman and I talked and arranged to meet up in London's West End.

I had heard about Norman and most of what I'd heard I didn't like. As it turned out, Norman had heard much about his interviewer and he didn't like that, either. But as we sat down, we were immediately drawn to each other's openness and honesty. Being the more public of the two, I was soon able to clear up misunderstandings that went round as a result of rumours. But Norman's past was not public news; it wasn't good news either. We met at midday and finished our lunch at 3.30. We continued talks over the infamous Perrier water and decided to stay for tea. At 5.30 pm the management asked us to leave!

Norman, a divorcee, had married Sheila. It was against the advice and wishes of several evangelical leaders. Norman would be the first to say that his behaviour before he met Sheila made a black sheep look positively saintly! After several years of marriage, they decided to sell their house in Croxley Green, Rickmansworth, and invest in Sheila's work, career and ministry. They had nowhere to live. They were invited to 52 Between Streets for four months. They stayed four years.

But that was not the end of it. The seven of us were to be together for seven years. Those first four years provided fellowship, friendship and a pastoral environment for Norman and Sheila. There were many pressures on the marriage, as a result of their travelling together, with Norman being both her friend and husband, as well as her manager. She was often misunderstood for things she said or did, and sometimes for the way she dressed. She was also a pioneer. But her work often took them abroad, which provided us with a little more space. But Norman and Sheila were family and it was difficult to think of the family without them.

Sheila toured the USA, the UK and other parts of Europe. Cliff Richard respected her both as a singer and a speaker. They toured together occasionally, which included South Africa. It was often suggested that I should speak at her concerts. This would have given me a ready-made platform. I certainly felt I had things to say, relevant things—some would even say, prophetic. But it didn't seem right. Sheila was a brilliant communicator in her own right and didn't need me. But she was of the same spirit, and the prophetic people of Bible times clearly sparked each other off. We did the same. I often felt she was able to say what was on my heart, but often said it better than I could have said it.

Cliff Richard and his Christian manager and friend, Bill Latham, had clearly been impressed by the pastoral care we had given Norman and Sheila. It wasn't easy for them being part of a household of seven people, with such an erratic and demanding life style. One day, Cliff brought Alvin Stardust and his wife, Liza Goddard, to a Cobham meeting I was speaking at. At the close, I called for a response and Alvin responded with tears in his eyes. But it is not easy being a committed believer, and being in the public eye—expectations are enormous, as are the temptations. When asked on a radio interview sometime later, 'Are you a Christian?', he replied, 'Yes—but not a good one.'

Nevertheless, the BBC had asked Sheila to host a series entitled *The Rock Gospel Show*. Although the show received good ratings, I found myself defending Sheila publicly and privately. Many Christians thought that Sheila was host, producer, director and adviser rolled into one. The BBC were keen to have Hindus and Muslims on the show, which resulted in not a few stormy meetings, as we sought to explain that there is a difference between Christians and Muslims!

The next series was co-hosted with Alvin. Every now and then, they were able to say something about their faith. But often the content was edited out. Viewers didn't realise that. Occasionally, I would sit in the studio and pray for her as the show was recorded. Those who speak for God have to speak to God—and it isn't always in public—much of it is private.

'Where there is no vision the people are un-
restrained.'

Proverbs 29:18 (NASB)

'Ideally, when Christians meet, as Christians to
take counsel together, their purpose is not—or
should not be—to ascertain what is the mind of
the majority but what is the mind of the Holy
Spirit—something which may be quite different.'

Margaret Thatcher, Prime Minister,
Summer 1989

Chapter 6

The Visionary (1980–1990)

So far, the prophet didn't seem to be prophesying very much, though everybody said I was prophetic. But I comforted myself that this had more to do with how I lived, than the continual 'Thus said the Lord' people expected.

It was at a prophetic conference where I was a speaker that the American worship leader, Wayne Drain, called me up on to the platform.

He took two tambourines and prophesied, 'Gerald, there have been tensions in your heart. You have been called to speak on God's behalf—you are a prophet. But you're also a bridge-builder—a reconciler among people. God is going to use you to bring the house churches and the music scene together. You'll be like the chain on a bicycle. People will use you, you'll often feel stretched and taut—but unless you're willing to do this, the two wheels of the house church movement and the Christian music industry will not move together.'

There was a general perception within the house church movement that the music industry was full of ambitious, independent people whose lives and marriages were in considerable need. In many cases, their assessments were not inaccurate. The music industry looked at the house churches and reckoned they were an introspective bunch of people, closed to anything their apostles didn't approve of. That wasn't too inaccurate, either.

Norman and I put together an event which we called, at Pete Meadows' suggestion, The Banquet. For a weekend in May of 1983, and again in 1984, Wembley Arena was filled with gospel bands, worship, teaching and evangelism. Speakers included David Watson, David Pawson, Eric Delve and myself. Singers included Sheila Walsh, Dave Pope, Andrae Crouch, Phil Keaggy, Dave Bilbrough, Dana and Cliff Richard.

At those two weekend events, hundreds came to Christ. Many were baptised in the Holy Spirit or returned to Christ after a period of backsliding. It was no longer possible to categorise the house churches and their agenda. Nor was it possible to pigeonhole all musicians. Sure, there were independent musicians whose marriages fell apart and who, despite their message, were not part of a body of believers. But it was also true that there was a multitude of house churches who'd come to the conclusion that their way of doing things was the best way—even the only way!

In 1985, The Banquet went on tour to twenty different towns and cities. Involved were Ishmael, well known for his 'praise parties', Donn Thomas, a cousin of Little Richard, who'd taken part in a previous Wembley Banquet, and relative newcomer Noel Richards. A strong prophetic challenge and call to holiness and repentance was issued to the thousands who attended. But where had Noel Richards come from?

An extremely exciting church had emerged in Plymouth, attracting a host of young people. According to the leadership team, they had invited several house church leaders to speak. Most had, in their estimation, wanted to take them over. I responded positively to an invitation to speak. Noel Richards, a member of the church, was a singer/songwriter/evangelist working with British Youth For Christ.

But the leader of the Plymouth church, having done a fabulous job with the group, was under increasing pressure. The sort of young people they were attracting were full of problems. Drugs, premarital sex and family problems were not unusual.

One day, he phoned my office in Cobham: 'I need help—I need it straight away.' As it happened, a trip had been planned for Plymouth. When I arrived, the story unfolded. The leader, exhausted, was taking to his bed. He would then give himself to the leadership of the church, meeting the many needs of the young people, teaching on Sundays and evangelising with the group. Exhausted, he'd go back to bed for a couple of days again. What was to be done? There was no other senior person who could take the church on.

So it was agreed that the family would go to Cobham. It would be for a few months, to recuperate, with a view to returning to Plymouth. The leadership team were called together in the evening and the proposal was put to them.

'Great,' they said, 'when do we move?'

The leadership obviously misunderstood. It was only the main leader and his family who would be moving to Cobham. It would be for a few months, they would still be financially supported from the Plymouth church—and then they'd return. But that is not how the leadership team saw it. They explained they couldn't go on like this—there was no one to lead their fellowship. Cobham were unable to supply anyone permanently. Upon return to Cobham, the story was shared with the Cobham leadership team.

One wisely commented, 'If the Plymouth fellowship

collapses, or if major problems emerge—the blame is going to rest with you.'

Another suggested, 'Let them come to Cobham, then at least we can keep our eye on things.' In the event, forty people moved home and jobs to settle in Cobham. The leader decided not to stay and moved away. There were just two or three others of the group who eventually moved on elsewhere.

Noel Richards, now in Cobham, left British Youth For Christ, and took a job. Later, he was invited by the church to work with me. He became a travelling companion, leading worship and singing songs. The rest of his time was spent taking missions in schools, colleges and universities, and in church work. Noel and I were to become best friends.

But the partnership produced more than simply friendship.

There is a close relationship between music and prophecy. When Saul met with the school of prophets, they were singing and playing their instruments and the question was asked, 'Is Saul also a prophet?' When Elisha was asked 'Is there a word from the Lord?', he called for a musician and then began to prophesy about a strategem for battle. Noel Richards was an accomplished musician, but he'd been locked up to a traditionalist evangelical mind-set.

Inevitably, traditional clichés were hinged to his music. I was no musician, nor a songwriter. But Noel listened to my talks, and began to write songs about things which burdened me. He would often quip, 'It's been said that I can sing in four minutes what it takes Gerald forty-five minutes to talk about!' His fine worship songs were not influenced by his mentor, though. They were mainly written with his wife, Trisha. 'Lord and Father, King for Ever', 'All Heaven Declares', 'You Laid Aside Your Majesty' and 'By Your Side I Will Stay', were all theirs.

So were the beautiful 'I Will Seek Your Face' and 'A Living Sacrifice'.

But there's no doubt that the songs Noel Richards was writing were prophetic, and it was not unusual for audiences to be in tears at concerts as the Holy Spirit touched them. Many were challenged by songs about AIDS, relationships, believing the best of people, and being lion-hearted and courageous.

Uniquely enough it was during this particular period of nine years that I began to prophesy prayerfully into situations, and some of the results seemed remarkable. The making of a prophet is more difficult than giving him words to prophesy. Glued on the inside front cover of my New American Standard Version of the Bible is a prayer of A. W. Tozer: '... Make my voice so like thine own that even the sick sheep will hear it and obey you.' Much had been done, but there was much more to do if I was to reach full potential and have a voice like our Lord's in tone and content. But I was a visionary and the vision kept me moving forward.

I was about to receive another vision, and a blow. It was Trish, Noel's wife, who had the picture: 'You were in a large auditorium and anybody who is anybody was there. I stood behind you, but there was a big gap between where I was standing and where you were standing. In front of us both there was this massive crowd, but all around you there was space. I tried to look into the space, but it was dark and misty. I thought to myself, "There are unseen things going on in that space."'

I took the vision to the leadership team and it was discussed. They felt that I should continue what I was doing with the Pioneer team: projects involving caring for churches, planting churches, training leaders through conferences and evangelists through TIE Teams

(Training in Evangelism). No one had any problems with my level of travel or with the content or style of my ministry. They felt they had to close the gap themselves.

I had an intuitive sense that something dark and serious was going to take place. A lady from a church in Surbiton told me, at the close of a meeting I was speaking at, 'I saw a stage, and there was another high stage behind it. The phrase "A parting of the ways" came to me—but you must stay on the high stage.' I had no idea what it meant, but I was about to learn.

By the early eighties I had been released from local responsibilities. A colleague doing a similar work to my own, Pete Lyne who lived in Bristol, asked to see me one day. We lunched at a pleasant hotel in Reading, equidistant between Bristol and London.

'Gerald,' Pete said, 'I think it's about time you gave up the leadership of the Cobham Fellowship and gave yourself to a wider, national ministry.' The words were simple. They affected me deeply. As I drove home, I hardly remember how I got back to Cobham. The only way I can describe the effect of his words was that the vehicle was filled with the Spirit of God.

How would the leaders at Cobham take it? Well, they took it well. Slowly but strategically I shifted from the local mix to give myself to a wider work and eventually put together a team from outside the area. One of my friends took over the leadership of the church with the full approval of all involved. He did an excellent job in keeping it on course, and it grew under his leadership. But some years later, he was getting bored and communicated that to several of his friends.

Ishmael, an exceptional leader among families and children, was on the Pioneer team. The team met monthly to share, pray and plan. At one meeting, Ishmael had a vision. It consisted of Mike behind the wheel of a car in a Grand Prix race. He went past the winning-line, with people cheering and clapping. As titles came up on the screen, it became clear that it was not the finish of the race, but of 'stage one—first leg'. It was clear Mike had come to the end of an era. He discussed it with me. Should he take a six-month break? Should he join John Noble's team? Should he plant another church? Scenarios were discussed, and one option was taken but never materialised.

Burn-out? Breakdown? These things are difficult to assess in the situation. Mike said he couldn't stay; he had come to the end of an era and while he was grateful for the church and his friends, he needed a fresh beginning elsewhere. It is true you hurt those you love the most, and it was to be true in this situation. He couldn't find his way into the will of God by staying with the Pioneer team or the network. He resigned from the leadership team and the church, and eventually moved away. Few really understood what Mike was going through and were themselves in a state of shock.

So I had lost another friend, and had to cancel a number of summer projects to fill in for him over the next few months. Martin Scott took over the role, though he was also in a state of depression for several months, as Mike had been such a help to him. There were many meetings when the entire leadership were in tears. Could we have done more? Mike had been in the church for over fifteen years. Why didn't we detect what was happening? But it was all too late. I would rather not record these events, yet without them I could be charged with writing as though I had a charmed life.

Depressed, and questioning my leadership role, I went with Noel to speak at a small Elim church in East London. One of the leaders, Cleland Thom, wrote afterwards: 'I saw you walking up and down in a large room. In the centre there was a table. On the table was an unfinished jigsaw puzzle. You were angry with yourself, angry with God and those around you. You were asking why you couldn't finish the jigsaw. You had a good idea of what it should look like, but you were unable to finish it. I saw you frustrated,' Clel explained, 'but after you'd raised your voice to God, there was silence. Then God spoke: "Son, you cannot possibly finish the jigsaw—I haven't given you all the pieces."'

There were pieces of the jigsaw I hadn't seen, people I hadn't met, probably people who weren't even converted yet, who would help me finish my part of the picture. It demanded fresh humility and dependence on God. The picture was to see Great Britain re-evangelised. It was June 1987. Just four weeks previously, Roger Forster, Lynn Green, Graham Kendrick and I had led 15,000 people through the City of London, praying for the nation. At that time, we had little idea what the City March for Jesus would develop into. The small flame was to become a roaring fire.

Another influence was a girl who occasionally wrote from the West Country, Joy Ryde. In September 1987, she had a picture of me sitting on the floor of a pleasantly decorated room, wearing a smart dark suit with lots of seemingly important papers scattered on the floor. My hair was in a conventional style. There was another person in the room, and a globe of the world. In the second part of the vision, she saw me dressed in a dark suit and carrying a brief-case with its important papers. I was going through the door of what appeared to be an airport. My appearance seemed to be that of a diplomat or ambassador. Whatever else I had been, it was certainly not a diplomat! But the woman's ministry had been tested before, and she should be taken seriously.

I rarely wore a suit; there had been a reaction against the suit-and-tie brigade. So it didn't seem very likely.

Danny Smith was leader of the 'Free the Siberian

Seven' campaign, which became the Jubilee Campaign, caring for the suffering church worldwide. The Pioneer Trust funded Danny to direct the work, and indirectly funded various Jubilee projects.

Russian evangelist Valeri Barinov had been jailed on several occasions and had been placed in a mental hospital for 'treatment'. He was a remarkable evangelist. On one occasion, Danny couldn't get hold of him. When contact was made, he enquired, 'Where have you been?'

Valeri replied, 'Oh, I was preaching outside the Museum of Atheism in Red Square. I was arrested and they put me in prison until I could pay a fine of fifty roubles.'

Danny paused, and then said, 'Valeri, that's terrible.'

Quick as a flash, Valeri replied, 'No, it isn't—it's wonderful. It would have cost me 300 roubles if I had had to hire a hall!'

David Alton MP had launched the Jubilee Campaign at the House of Commons with Danny and myself. Almost 100 MPs—a quarter of the House—would campaign for prisoners-of-faith throughout the world. After the strong campaign, Valeri Barinov and his family were given permission to come to Britain. But Danny was nervous. Others had an interest in being identified with the success of the campaign.

In discussion with Danny, I cancelled a weekend of meetings, something I'd never done in almost twenty years of full-time ministry. We received a message that Valeri and his family were on a plane bound for Heathrow. We had already raised funds through a colleague at CARE Trust, Lyndon Bowring, to fly the family out of Russia. We had also been to see Brian Phillips at Elm House Publications and, in association with *Christian Family* magazine, agreed to raise funds for a home for the Barinovs.

That Sunday I spent all day on the phone. I dealt with

many phone calls which Danny felt he couldn't handle because of a complicated mix in both national and international affairs. In dressing-gown and bare feet, I talked and listened for hours to various parties. Anona pushed a plate of bacon and eggs under my nose. 'Fine Sunday lunch this is,' I thought. When all was done, I had less than an hour to get to Heathrow and present myself to David Alton, Danny Smith, television cameras and the national press. I put a wet brush through my hair, which was normally spiked with gel (I thought it took a few years off my looks!), put on something smart, and grabbed my brief-case full of mail.

Rush hour on the M25 is a contradiction in terms. But the road was remarkably clear. Upon arriving, I parked the car, ran across to the main terminal and as I entered the airport doors, the hair on the back of my neck went up. There I was in a dark-grey suit and a shirt and tie, with my hair dried-out and 'conventional', not spiked as it was normally. In my hand was a brief-case full of important papers—some to do with Valeri's arrival. The vision had become a reality.

Valeri and his family were on the plane. He settled in Cobham for a year, and later went to America to work for a while and eventually purchased a property on the south coast.

From then on, I began to wear jacket and tie, or suits, more regularly. On one occasion, I walked into a 'new church' situation. Three young men roared with laughter. 'A suit—a suit! Where's the funeral?'

I looked them up and down and noted how they were dressed. 'I don't know,' I replied; 'where's the jumble sale?'

Terry Page, who led a Shaftesbury Centre in Chiswick, South West London, spoke with me at a conference at the close of 1987. Before him he held a picture that had been on the wall of the room. 'You can see before you a silvery river running through a seemingly barren wilderness. This is the area God has called you to. Slopes are on the left and on the right. These are the work-faces of Pioneer, your work in Britain, South Africa, Uganda, Jubilee, the AIDS initiative ACET, and March for Jesus. The work-faces are dusty, dirty and hard work. God wants to draw your attenton away from the grime and towards the river, which has cut through the land for years. You are a hard worker but you must not get too hung up with the tasks God has given you. You need to put your tools down at times. Stop your work. Bathe in the river. Rest and be still—wash yourself clean. God wants you to do this every day—even several times a day—for long periods of time. He is the stream in the valley.'

From then on, I set aside regular days to think, pray and listen to the Lord.

So visions, pictures and prophecies had guided, steered, motivated and hemmed me in to God's will. Where would I have been without them? But what about my desire to be a voice for God?

It was Blaise Pascal who said, 'The stream is always purer at its source.' I wanted to get nearer the source. I was convinced that the sourcc has pure and appropriate words for people and peoples. God's will is in his word. God's will is never found outside of his word. His word is utterly reliable and toally dependable. That is why evangelical Christians have such a high view of Scripture.

But the God who has spoken is the God who still speaks. Although evangelicals and church people in general talk about the God who speaks, it is often based more on odd feelings than anything else. People feel 'led' to do things for God. My friend Rodney Kingstone put it well when he commented, 'Too many people have got felt-led poisoning!'

But it was obvious that the God who spoke must still

speak. There is not the slightest indication in Scripture to lead us to believe that God has nothing more to say than what he has already said. Of course, what he is saying is based upon what he said, and cannot contradict it. For God's will is in his word.

There were clearly many prophecies given in New Testament times which Scripture does not record. So not everything that the Spirit prompts people to say has been canonised.

In 1984, Luis Palau came to London for an evangelistic mission. It was held at Queens Park Rangers' football ground. BBC's *Everyman* programme decided to film the meetings, interview Luis, speak to his converts and then make their assessments. It was to be shown at peak viewing time, not in a religious slot.

The meetings were in full swing when I received a phone call from another member of the organising Executive. 'We're in trouble. A thief has stolen the BBC vehicle, complete with cameras, sound-equipment and—for us, worst of all—the film.'

The Holy Spirit leaped within me. I said to Anona, 'We need to pray for this—I've got faith that God is going to do something.'

It wasn't long before the phone rang again. This time it was Pete Meadows, the Chief Executive of the Mission to London. 'You've heard about the film, Gerald—well, at the close of the meeting we'd like you to pray that we'll get the film back.'

That night the platform was filled with thirty or more people. After Dave Pope had led the singing, there had been one or two stories of people who had become Christians, and Sheila Walsh sang. Luis Palau preached well. There was a great response at the close, and hundreds became Christians. I was ushered to the microphone, briefly explained what had happened and prayed.

'Father, in the light of what we've heard this evening, we ask that you will ensure these cans of film are brought back into the right hands, so that we can see Luis Palau, and what you're doing here, on our national television screens.'

I then went off to Germany, where I was due to speak at meetings with my friend, Norman Barnes, who runs Links International; this organisation does precisely what its name conveys, linking leaders and churches together throughout the nations.

Sitting in a square in Hanover, I was reading about the York Minster fire, the Bishop of Durham and his denial of Scripture and creed. I thought it was fascinating that church leaders within the Anglican communion defended Dr Jenkins, while godless newspaper editors made it clear that if you play around with God, you shouldn't be surprised to get your fingers (or your cathedral roofs) burned!

Upon our arrival back in Cobham, I received a call. 'You're in trouble with the BBC!' I was baffled.

'Why?' I enquired.

'Because they've only got the film back!'

The thief had driven back to the football ground, deposited the film at the turnstiles and driven off again. As far as I know the BBC never did see their vehicle, the cameras or the sound-equipment again. Some weeks later, Luis Palau, the Mission to London and the wonderful number of converts were seen on our television screens.

'Ask and you shall receive': a prophetic statement for prophetic prayers?

R. T. Kendall was the man who had the unenviable task of stepping into the shoes of Dr Martyn Lloyd-Jones at Westminster Chapel. R.T. is a precise, sincere but fairly strait-laced Bible teacher, much in demand throughout the United Kingdom and overseas. He had spoken at the Leadership 84 conference organised by the Evangelical Alliance, on changes in his church, explaining how he had defied the tradition of his church by taking to the streets every Saturday to 'win souls for Christ'.

At the close of the meeting, I was in tears. 'I just felt I wanted to go out and find a street full of people and tell them about Jesus,' I commented to friends. I needed to be alone.

Walking back to the chalet, I met Clive Calver, General Secretary of the Evangelical Alliance—a good friend. 'Are you OK?' he enquired, with obvious care.

'Oh, yes—I've been deeply moved by what R.T. has said today,' I replied.

'Well, that's interesting, because he's just asked if he can meet you.'

The two of us walked to R.T.'s chalet, knocked on the door and were ushered in. Seated to our right was a well-known Reformed minister whose church tradition was non- if not anti-charismatic. R.T. and I put our arms round each other. 'It was love at first sight,' R.T. was to say quite publicly in leadership meetings.

Soon, an invitation came for dinner at the Kendalls' home in Ealing, the former home of Martyn Lloyd-Jones ('the doctor'). Anona and I prayed as we drove up the A3, through Richmond Park and into Ealing: 'Dear God, please don't let us get into theology this evening.' R.T. was a Calvinist, but I reckoned I could drive a fleet of buses through Calvinism. I was not a Calvinist, but I reckoned R.T. could drive a fleet of buses through my theology. The difference was that, as far as theology was concerned, R.T. was a better driver than me!

Upon arrival, R.T. gave us the kind of welcome we like! We were given a short tour of the house and then taken to the dining-room. We gave thanks for the meal, and R.T. looked up, asking, 'Can we have a nice, light evening?' Our prayers had been answered. His next question was, 'Do you think a Christian can have a demon?' Heavens, I thought, and this is a nice, light evening!

Now, when a Calvinist asks you a question like that, they don't want your latest experience or dramatic stories. They want chapter and verse, a broad biblical exegesis and the place in the maps where it happened! Before we had time to answer, R.T. said, 'Do you know, I've got the two most demonised people I've ever seen in all my life—in my church.' We had never been to Westminster Chapel, didn't know anybody who went to it, and didn't even know where it was.

God then gave me a picture and two names. 'Are their names John and Myrtle?' I asked. (These weren't the names God gave me, but in the interests of confidentiality they'll do for now!)

R.T. nearly spat his prawns across the table. 'How did you know that?' he spluttered.

Afterwards, R.T. took us into another room. 'Do you know, you and another Christian leader are bringing about the biggest theological shift in my entire ministry,' he said. R.T. was gracious enough to receive our counsel.

But prophets sound braver than they really are. The fear of making a mistake, getting it wrong in public, dishonouring the name of the Lord, and just being made to look plain silly have run through the most courageous heart. But curiosity overcame fear. Well, at least most of the time.

I was curious to know how far God would go in unfolding 'words of knowledge'. It was clear that God knew a great deal, and to drop a few words into a heart or mind was no great problem for the almighty God who created the cosmos. But fears still lodged here and there.

Noel Richards and I had a series of meetings in

Cheshire. The first was a youth night. But this was a raw youth night. There were no airs and graces here. Noel gave me the sort of look that said quite simply: How did this event get in our diary?

'You take the meeting,' I suggested. But Noel declined. 'I'm happy to do it, but you have been advertised as the speaker.'

I was desperate. I felt I had nothing to say. These kids could see through anything that was put on for the evening. I was old enough to be their father. Noel did a great job in grabbing their attention, singing songs and making a platform for me.

We all pray best under pressure, and I was under pressure. 'Lord, what do you want to do this evening?'

With that, the door opened and the Lord spoke: 'That boy's name is Mark.'

I'd once heard, on tape, a prophet of God give out the family details of someone's life and then ask, 'Do you believe God can heal you?' But this was now—and it was with me! What if his name was George, or Fred, or Dagnal! I launched into my talk, feeling very insecure and hopelessly out of place.

Two-thirds of the way through, I chickened out, but pointed to the young man who'd come in the door. Needing a visual aid, I asked the boy, 'And what's your name?'

'Mark,' he replied.

I was so angry with myself. I asked to see Mark and his friends after the meeting. I explained they had no way of knowing whether what I was about to say was true or not true. I explained they were unlikely ever to see me again.

'Guys, I want to apologise to you,' I said. 'I didn't want to do tonight. I felt I was the least-equipped in the hall to speak to you all. In desperation, I asked God for some help and when you came in, Mark, God told me who you were and what your name was. I think if I'd pointed you out in the meeting and said, "I know your name is Mark, God knows your name is Mark; what do you want God to do for you?", the whole meeting would have blown open with folk responding to the need of salvation and faith in Christ. But I failed. And I want to apologise to you. I let you down and, more importantly, I let God down.'

A deep sense of reverence filled the area where we were standing. One or two, deeply moved, experienced tears filling their eyes. I went back to the home I was staying in, disappointed with myself.

The next night, we were in a converted cinema. This time, a lot of prayer and thought had gone into the talk! As Noel led the worship, I nervously asked the Lord if there was anything he particularly wanted to do that night. 'Yes, Gerald, there's another Mark here.'

Grief, I thought to myself, I'm making it up now! 'Lord, you show me where he's sitting, and I promise I'll respond this time.'

I took out a piece of paper, quickly drew a plan of the cinema, and sensed the Lord was asking me to put a cross at the top left-hand block of seats. I wrote the name 'Mark' by it.

Three-quarters of the way through the talk, I said, 'There's a Mark here tonight. I want you to stand.' At the top, in the left-hand block, a single man stood amidst several hundreds. He came, as requested, down to the front. I showed him the piece of paper and asked, 'What do you want God to do for you?'

The appeal that followed created a phenomenal response, with many coming to faith and being visibly moved with the power of God. Bodies were lying all around the front of the meeting, having been touched by God—often not by me at all.

As we drove home, I turned to the host, John

Cavanagh. Somewhat relieved, I thanked God for a wonderful evening, particularly in the light of the failure the night before. 'Oh, it was a lot more wonderful than you think,' John commented. 'That young man, Mark, was sitting in the front of the meeting while you were writing all that down. After you put the piece of paper in your pocket, for some reason he moved and went and sat up at the back.' Wonderful indeed!

Some while later, Noel and I were at the well-known Millmead Centre in Guildford, overseen at the time by Fred Elgar. The eldership team had asked me to speak to some sixty or more people involved in pastoral care at an early morning learning centre. I then spoke at the main morning meeting to some 600 people. We were asked to speak on the subject of holiness, and I spoke about holiness of character and holiness of service. I told my story about Mark and how I had failed, and what to do when you've failed, in holy service.

As I continued speaking, I pointed to a young man— the only person I chose to address out of 600 who were present. 'God sees the pressure you are under, young man, the times you've been alone, the questions you are asking and how God is discipling you in circumstances beyond your control. But you are in his will.'

At the close of the meeting, the young man came up to me and said, 'Thanks for that—you don't know how helpful it was. By the way, my name is Mark!' Fred Elgar went to the microphone and explained what had happened.

That night, another packed auditorium at Millmead saw a great response at the close of the meeting. Many came forward for salvation, for the fullness of the Holy Spirit, and to reaffirm their commitment to Christ and his purposes.

The last couple to come forward were both dressed in green sweaters. 'You may have been the last to come down, but you might like to know that green is God's favourite colour,' I joked. I then went on to say, 'You're just about to make major changes in your life; I see major decisions ahead of you in the immediate period of time before you. It has to do with the man but it involves the woman as well. You must understand that God is going to look after you, my dear, as well as your husband.'

She burst into tears. They then explained that they were just about to go off to Bible College and were giving up their jobs, and that she felt she was doing much of it, albeit with a good conscience, for him.

One or two words, pictures and prophecies of this nature would be a regular feature of meetings with leaders, in church meetings and at special events. On several occasions the Lord would help me to speak over someone in a hall containing several hundred people and, afterwards, point to someone on the other side of the hall and put them together. It was not unusual for them to be brothers, best friends or even father and son, as happened once at Reading Leisure Centre.

God gave me a word for a man in the third row, who looked as though he was in his early sixties. Six or seven hundred people were present. In the second-to-back row, some twenty or more rows from the front, God then gave a word for a young man whom I spoke with after the meeting. I explained to the young man, privately, that God wanted to do something important with his father. I asked whether the father was a Christian. I was told that he was, and that he was actually in the meeting.

I was a little surprised at this, but was totally unprepared for the next line: 'Yes, in fact he was the man you prophesied over at the front.'

I called them together. They prayed with each other and wept over each other.

Although I enjoy speaking and developing skills as an orator, a life touched here and there by God's Spirit is what really makes everything worth while. But I knew I was scratching the surface, and needed to get even closer to the source.

We all see life through our ministry. If a church isn't growing, pastors feel it needs more pastoral care. Teachers feel it needs more Bible teaching. Prophets know it needs the word of the Lord!

Prophetic words are sometimes a kick in the intellect to conservative evangelicals.

Danny Smith had been heading up the 'Free the Siberian Seven' campaign. He had also been instrumental in securing their release, along with thirty or more others. Indeed, he had succeeded where other Christian leaders and politicians had failed. A 'thank you' meeting was arranged for people within the Pioneer network and others who had prayed for the Chmykalov family. Timothy Chmykalov came to the meeting. There was praise and prayer, and then Timothy spoke.

At the close of the meeting, I asked Danny Smith and his wife, Joan, to come to the platform. Several gathered round to pray for them. 'Danny and Joan, you've worked hard and you have many friends all over the country as a result of your work. But this is a time for you to find out who your real friends are,' I prayed. There was no 'Thus said the Lord' or anything of that nature. But both Danny and Joan wept profusely. I wondered why. They lived in North London. It turned out that all the way down the A3 to Guildford, where the meeting was being held, they were discussing issues of home, church and who were their 'real friends'.

Through that experience, they sold their house, moved to Cobham and were partly funded by the Pioneer Trust. It seemed such a simple word to give. But when a few words have been revealed, anointed and communicated, they can change a world. Danny would change several worlds.

Dr Patrick Dixon worked in terminal care. He was a part of the Ealing Christian Fellowship. The main leader, John Spencer, is now the Chairman of the Pioneer Trust. Patrick was often frustrated with the somewhat cautious, laid-back style that had marked the steady growth of the church. It was the mid-eighties, and 100 Pioneer leaders were at one of their spring conferences. After the conference, I was clearing up, along with Noel Richards, Pioneer administrator Rob Dicken, and one or two helpers.

Dr Dixon was in tears. He told me, 'I find this so difficult to believe. I thought God would speak to the Ealing leadership.' Clearly, he felt called to be a leader, was willing to give up his job, and in order to lead the fellowship, was willing to make the sacrifice. It was just a matter of others seeing it. They didn't. The Ealing elders were going home encouraged and challenged, but there were no major changes.

'Patrick,' I told him, 'you're never going to lead the Ealing Christian Fellowship. You have leadership skills, but they lie outside of a local church. I feel it has something to do with your medical work, but I'm not into medicine so I can't tell you more than that.'

As I drove home, I wondered what that was all about. It seemed such a foolish thing to say. Penicillin had been invented! What was he going to do that would fulfil this call to lead?

As a result of caring for those with terminal cancer, Dr Dixon also came across those who were dying of AIDS. Something had to be done. What should he do? A deal was agreed, and Patrick wrote a book. On November 5th 1987, at the press launch of *The Truth About AIDS*, we both launched a practical care and education initiative; it was called quite simply Pioneer for AIDS.

In January 1988, Pioneer Trust took on Brian Harris, who had worked with evangelist Eric Delve. We only had eight weeks' salary in the bank, a shared telephone, a Post Office box number and a thousand letterheads. It was another step of faith. Patrick's book had been widely received, and John Stott would quote favourably from it in a future publication. A press conference at the Barbican went well. But while Brian was setting up the organisation, Patrick was still frustrated.

Later that month, we began to train the first fifty home-care volunteers. Through a mutual friend, Paul Bennison in Rustington, we were put in touch with World in Need, a Christian trust which launched Help the Aged. Senior people at World in Need had read Patrick's book.

Eight weeks of intensive negotiations followed, at the end of which we both agreed to change the name to give a broader appeal. An expanded group of trustees was created and the new charity, ACET (AIDS Care Education and Training), was launched. It retained all the original vision, the historic links and relationships. I spend a day a month as an adviser to Patrick and ACET. The Pioneer network of relationships has acted as a base for training, and the creation of various ACET centres. The initiative is relational, not institutional.

By 1990, ACET had around thirty staff working in four major centres around the country, providing home-care for more men, women and children suffering from HIV (AIDS) than any other charity. ACET was also the country's largest independent provider of AIDS-prevention classes in schools.

In partnership with Tear Fund, it launched an AIDS programme in Uganda. Three exploratory trips had already been made.

As World in Need's funding in this country began to phase out, it was replaced by health authorities, local councils, central government, trusts, companies, churches and individual donors.

Those few prophetic words at the conference centre in Sussex, years previously, had borne fruit. God's will is in his word.

If a few apparently innocuous words to a Danny Smith or a Patrick Dixon could help launch or sustain international initiatives—what could be done to reach a nation? Again, it had to start with a person.

It was in Belfast, in the early part of 1990, that Noel Richards and I were invited to a series of meetings at the Christian Fellowship Church led by Paul Reid. In the course of the series, teaching and perspectives were given to city-wide leaders, a broad leadership team of the church, and to one or two newly-planted churches. There were also a couple of evening conference meetings. But at the close of one meeting, after an appeal, I handed it over to Paul. Although there were 600 people present, I sensed God was directing me to the back row again!

I left the platform and walked to the back. I tapped a young man on the shoulder and said, 'God has shown me you have a cloud over you. It's not of your own doing, it's not sin—even though we're all sinners. This is going to be used to have your prayers answered. You've prayed some pretty big prayers.'

Tears filled the young man's eyes. How could the speaker of the conference know this? He'd been speaking from the stage, almost 100 feet away. But it was true. He told me, 'On Monday of this week, the IRA shot my cousin. I've just flown from Aberdeen University for the funeral today. I just thought I'd come along tonight.' The young man left encouraged and blessed by God's attention and his servant's words.

A few of God's choice words, touching the lives of choice people could change things for ever. But a nation?

On the first of our trips to Uganda, Dr Dixon, Noel Richards, Martin Scott, black Ugandan Anthony Kazozi and I found ourselves in the home of Dr Balaki Kyria, Minister of State to the President's office and Chief of Security. A wonderful Christian, he opened the Scriptures regarding the Second Coming and we prayed together. He was a courteous host. As we prayed, God gave me another of the precious few visions I've ever had.

I'd asked the Lord many times, 'How do you touch a nation?' The prophets in the Bible seemed to have the right word for the right people, and God gave them access to key leaders. It happened that Dr Kyria, one of the most senior men in the country, was a member of the church my team were speaking to. But now I was nervous. What if I was making it up? What if it was my imagination? This was a specific vision. If it wasn't of God, it wouldn't happen and I would lose credibility. We would probably be denied access again. If it was of God, and I didn't share it—what would happen?

As the party left, I shuffled around, pretending to take an interest in certain things in the house. Dr Kyria and I were left alone in the room. I said to him, 'Dr Kyria, you don't know me—you may never see me again. But I've had a vision, sir. It is of your home surrounded by hostile troops; they are staging some sort of coup. With respect, sir, I believe you need to increase the security on your property and that of other government ministers and offices.'

Dr Kyria looked me straight in the eyes. 'Thank you, young man. I shall give that attention.' I liked the 'young man' bit, though at the time I was forty-three!

Just a few weeks later, hundreds of armed troops

stormed government buildings. Shortly afterwards, Dr
Kyria moved house, security was tightened and the
country made more secure. Members of the presidential
family had found faith, as had other government ministers over that period of time. Mr Mussevini and many of
his ministers wanted to bring Christian ethics, values
and morals into the nation.

The then Minister of Education, Mr Joshua Mayanja-
Akanji, told the team, 'Tell my students about AIDS and
Jesus—but most of all, tell them about Jesus.' To go into
schools and colleges with the gospel, and a health
message authorised personally by the Minister of
Education opened door after door for us. Hundreds
responded to the good news about Jesus.

We live in an age where style is often more important
than substance. Some liked my prophetic style—others
most certainly did not.

One who did was Wesley Shelbourne. His father had
started a Pentecostal church in the city of Lincoln,
twenty-five years prior to a remarkable event. He was an
evangelist. His name was John and he was widely
respected in Assemblies of God circles. Another 'new
church' had sprung up in Lincoln many years later. The
two leaders, John Shelbourne and Stuart Bell, believed
that God was wanting the two churches in the city to be
one.

Blending two mature ministries together is not easy,
and it wasn't without its tensions and pressures. Stuart
Bell was eventually given leadership of the church, now
called the New Life Centre, with a team including
singer/songwriter Chris Bowater and Bible teacher John
Phillips. It grew in size and influence.

John was at something of a loss. Every major change
is a crisis of self-esteem. His friends were at the New
Life Centre in Lincoln, but he didn't have the same

leadership role as before. His preaching, particularly around the nation and overseas was excellent, but he loved his family and didn't want to be away for too long.

Martin Scott, Noel and I were invited to lead a Lincoln celebration event attended by almost 1,000 people. Stuart Bell had become a good and close friend after we were invited to speak at his annual Grapevine event on two occasions. At the close of the meeting, Wesley was one of almost 100 who responded to prayer and ministry.

God gave me a prophetic word for Wesley. 'You've grown up in the shadow of your father. It isn't your fault, and it isn't your father's fault. Your father's a big man in every sense of the word—in size, in stature and in influence.'

John, his father, was sitting at the back of the meeting! Indeed, he had been to a series of seminars we had held throughout the day. Several had commented on John's open-eyed, eager response to our ministry. He was at every session and was now at the evening meeting— almost unprecedented.

I continued, 'Your father is what he is by God's grace; that's how God has made him. You've grown up under his shadow. But now you're about to become your own man. You're about to step out of the shadow. You're going to make your father very happy. He's going to look—as it were from heaven—and say, "This is my son with whom I am well pleased."' By now Wesley had sunk to his knees in tears, and John was deeply moved.

Seven days later, at the age of fifty-five, John went to be with the Lord. Wesley cherished the word from God. It was a preparation that was quite unexpected. From that moment on, Wesley blossomed, flourished and began to travel with Stuart Bell. He became a good friend. He would make his father happy? Yes. He would look 'as it were from heaven'? We shall see!

The kingdom of God is not like the political kingdoms and human empires we create.

Who would have thought that two thousand years ago, without radio, television, telephone or satellite communication, the teachings of Jesus would cover the nations of the earth? It was a miracle here, a few words of encouragement and direction given over there. Signs and wonders were, it seems, performed in a haphazard fashion in isolated instances. Not once is it ever mentioned that Jesus asked the disciples to record either his teaching or his history. He knew, however, he could trust the Holy Spirit to do what he didn't do!

The Intelligent Fire had lit a prophetic flame. This also worked in a haphazard, apparently unrelated, fashion.

When I was alone one day, the Lord spoke to me. 'Son, all you have ever said, you have been willing to say. You know someone somewhere has to say these things. But now I want to ask you, "Will you speak for me and say things you don't want to say?"' My eyes filled with tears. What would God want me to say that I would rather not say? I was about to find out.

It started in the middle of a talk at a celebration and teaching event in Surrey. 'There are two people here in an adulterous relationship. I don't mean flirtation, masturbation or gratification by contemplation. If you come clean tonight, God will forgive you and grant you a new beginning.' No one responded. Perhaps I looked silly or wrong. Days later the truth was out.

It was the pastor who had invited us to the meeting. On the night, he sat six feet behind us. His secretary, the other party involved, sat on the front row. There was no repentance and the pastor's marriage broke up. Had I failed to carry the word through?

I walked into a Cobham elders' meeting, the Spirit of God came upon me. I looked at Nigel Day, who had come from Plymouth. I literally heaved for a few moments and then wept. Martin Scott, the leader, and other elders had seen it before on occasion. They knew something special was about to be said. To Nigel it was a little unusual.

I said to him, 'Something is going to happen to you, Nigel. You aren't going to feel good about it. The enemy is setting you up. You need to prepare yourself for a shock, for something which is traumatic. You don't need to look for it, you will know it when it happens.'

I met with the elders for a strategy day every three months. Every time I saw Nigel, I felt the same. Nigel had been a communist and a 'moonie'. These things didn't satisfy him, and he turned to Christ. He had been a Christian for about fifteen years.

He had an excellent job, a company car and an offer of a place on the board. After prayer and discussion, the eldership team asked if he would lay his career aside, and give himself to working with Stuart Lindsell and Martin Scott, in the church in Cobham and its church-plants. That very week, he was offered promotion, a pay rise and 'everything I have ever wanted'. Was this the fulfilment of the prophecy? 'No, it isn't; it will be something far more traumatic than this,' I had to tell our leaders.

A few weeks later, a letter came. Nigel opened it with interest. He didn't recognise the handwriting or the postmark. The message was simple. He had a son whom he had not seen since he was a baby. He was now seventeen years of age, and wanted to meet his father! There could be few things more traumatic than that! I wrote to Nigel, 'I know that when you see him, you will be proud of him!'

Nigel had to face the issue on his own. He saw his son and apologised for events preceding and surrounding the birth. 'I felt quite proud of him,' he wrote to me afterwards. Friendship began to grow between Nigel and his son, and also between Nigel and me. Nigel had been prepared by the word from God; he was likely to trust my future intuition and words from the Lord.

Realising that life in the age to come must in some degree be an extension of the life we now live, I wondered if it would be possible to read anything then. God has committed himself to words. Jesus is the Word—but he hasn't yet had the last word. At the resurrection of the church and the judgement of the nations, he will have his last word—certainly as far as this age is concerned.

But it would appear from Scripture that the end of the age will be marked by a bride, adorned and preparing herself for the bridegroom; or, to change the analogy, a light shining in darkness. It would appear from Jesus' teaching that the light will get brighter and the darkness will get more evil and fearful. The essence of drama is conflict, and the conflict of the ages will be fought out before our Lord's return.

I have always thought it was a somewhat shallow interpretation of Scripture to tell Christians across the world who are being imprisoned, tortured and separated from their families that they wouldn't be going through the great Tribulation. But if the darkness is to get darker and the violence more violent, the only way the light can get brighter is by a greater outpouring of the Holy Spirit creating a fresh commitment to God, his word and his ways. Some call it revival.

Around this time, I was in New Zealand with my friends Richard Burt and Noel Richards. Peter Lyne from Bristol was now living in Auckland and had set up an excellent itinerary in the North Island for three weeks. Youth events with a thousand young people, celebration events with a similar number and several national media opportunities synchronised wonderfully.

But one morning, a small leadership event was arranged with no more than sixty men and women. Singer/songwriters Dave and Dale Garratt were leading worship. 'This is quite a *Who's Who*—we've never seen all these people in the same room together at one time,' they said. Clouds of pressure descended on me. Who had they come to see? What had they come to see? What did they expect to hear?

After a brief, warm introduction from Christian leader Wilbur Wright, I worked through the nervousness by sharing a little of my history, along with some throw-away lines and humorous anecdotes. Having steadied my nerves, I then attempted to get into my subject, 'The Two Priorities of Heaven,' which I felt was relevant to the meeting. I needed a bridge.

Suddenly, I found myself saying, '... and back home right now, we're preparing for revival.' And then I burst into tears. Somewhat embarrassed, I regained my equilibrium and carried on with what Dave Garratt thought was a most helpful talk. Indeed, the Garratts asked for a copy of it and they sent it out on their worldwide mailing list.

But what were these tears? Why on earth, in such a low-key gathering, did this happen? I thought about the phrase a great deal: 'back home, we're preparing for revival'!

I had met John Wimber as a result of giving a prophetic word to a friend, telling that friend that his music business would open up in America. The friend met John Wimber, and subsequently each gave the other the rights to distribute the other's music and worship songs in their respective countries. 'You must meet Gerald Coates,' the director of the music company told John: 'He prophesied this would happen.' When John was next over in London, we met quite 'by accident' and enjoyed one or two meals together.

There was occasional correspondence and warm greetings sent to each other through mutual friends, but that was about all. It was now 1990. John Wimber's relationship with Paul Cain and a prophetic school was becoming well known. Controversy was fanned by genuine concern, selfish interest, insecurity and anti-charismatic reaction.

Roger and Faith Forster, leaders of the Ichthus Christian Fellowship in South East London, felt they ought to go to a prophetic conference led by these men. Roger discussed it with his local leaders and with me. It was agreed they should go.

Almost immediately upon his return from America, Roger phoned me and explained that he had met Paul Cain and John Wimber, and that Paul had asked him to stand up in a meeting of over 4,000 people. Paul had also said that Anne Watson should stand beside Roger and Faith (something which I thought was significant). He had gone on to say that God had been speaking to him about a work of the Spirit which would be greater than anything that had been seen before in the British Isles, and that it would cover England and Wales. He had told Roger that he, along with a small network of brothers who were working with him, was 'being prepared for revival'.

Immediately Roger uttered those words, I began to heave and weep. It was exactly the same experience as with Nigel Day and several other people I'd prophesied over. The only other experience of this deep crying was when God showed me that there would be an earthquake in New Zealand, naming both the place where it would happen and the time it would happen. I shared this with a few key leaders in New Zealand, to prepare them. It is stored on tape.

In the book of Amos we are told that God never does anything unless he first reveals it to his servants 'the prophets'. Prophecy should not, as the apostle Peter said many hundreds of years later, be by private interpretation. There is a plurality about God and it is expressed in local church leadership and apostolic teams. So it should be with prophetic words.

But from various parts of the world, revival was on people's agendas. Could it happen in Britain? What sort of leaders would we need? Would the competitiveness, denominational superiority and small-mindedness of many leaders simply be magnified in a revival situation? Perhaps a new sort of leadership was needed: something that was primarily concerned with the kingdom of God, and with truth above and beyond, or even separate from, denominational loyalties. The name of the denomination nearly always marks the spot where the revelation stopped.

One night, I had been asked to speak to a couple of hundred teenagers in Surrey. At the close, I had an appeal; many responded and as we prayed, a few were in tears. I pointed to one young man who looked as though he was about sixteen. 'I know you come from the Cobham Fellowship, and although we've never had a single private conversation in our lives, I want to say to you publicly in front of all these people what I said to you a few weeks ago in front of your father. You and I are going to work together.'

As soon as I had said it, God showed me something. I went on, 'You had a supernatural birth. God saved you from death when you were born. The first few years of your life were not easy. Seven years ago, you were traumatised. But God is going to use these last seven years to shape you up for what lies ahead.' By now he was in tears. I looked at him, and perhaps in a moment of insecurity, added, 'These things are true, aren't they?' He nodded. I went home to Anona that night and explained what had happened.

'I'm sure that can't be right, dear,' she replied. 'I know the family well, and I think I would have known if something like that had happened.'

A few days later, I received a letter from the boy's mother. They had been in the Cobham Fellowship for several years. Then they had moved away. They had been left some property, but things didn't work out, either with the property or their business. So they made the courageous move, and indeed the right move, to come back to Cobham. It was a mark of their own integrity. They could have gone anywhere else in the nation, or abroad. Linda was American and still had many friends there. But the church was now large and I was nearly always away, so I hardly knew an entire family.

As it turned out, the boy, Nathan, had gone home and explained to his parents what had happened. He mentioned the 'birth' incident. 'What did he say about the birth? Tell us what he said about the birth!' Linda exclaimed, somewhat excitedly. You see, they had never told him, and when he nodded to me it was out of politeness.

Linda's lengthy letter, précised here, tells the story:

Dear Gerald,
I am writing in response to the prophetic word you had for Nathan. Obviously, he found the whole thing absolutely thrilling. I had a difficult fourteen-hour labour with Nathan. By the time he was born, both he and I were heavily drugged. I was hardly aware of anything during the delivery, and it wasn't until eight years later that Richard [her husband] told me of just what had occurred.

Nathan was born blue and not breathing. It was fifteen

minutes before he breathed. He was then supposed to
have been put into intensive care, but the message never
got through and it wasn't until several days later that the
mistake was discovered. At the time of Nathan's birth,
August 25th 1974, the Cobham Fellowship was away on
holiday. My husband told a family of the traumatic birth
and they agreed I should not be told, as they felt I
wouldn't be able to cope with any more.

Nathan did not get on very well at school. He simply
wasn't learning. He went to Downside, Parkside, Cobham
First and Cobham Middle. When he was eight, we were
told he was nothing but a lazy, deceptive child. Eventually,
Richard told me of Nathan's birth. We told a few of our
friends about it, but we didn't tell Nathan, as we didn't
want him to feel 'subnormal' in any way.

So Nathan started at a small prep. school of under a
hundred boys. He went in at the bottom of the school.
Teachers say his progress was amazing. On the first day
at school, he came first in a cross-country run. On his
second day, he was selected for the Colts football team.
He was put forward for a scholarship at Seaford College.

There, he was given the art scholarship and the sports
scholarship, and once he started at the school, he was
named a choir scholar. Teachers have said that Nathan
stands out from other boys. Teachers who are not
Christians say they would like to see Nathan do something
wrong for once!

Since he was a baby, I have prayed that he would be
great in the kingdom of God and that he would be in full-
time ministry. Over the weekend, the story of Samuel has
come separately to Richard and me. As Hannah gave
Samuel to Eli, so we want to give Nathan to you. We don't
know just how this will work out. But we want you to
know that we freely give Nathan to you, to prepare him
for the ministry of the gospel and all that would entail.
Love Linda and Richard.

I sat in bed that morning drinking coffee and reading
mail. As I read that letter, I wept and wept. It was

precisely seven years ago that he had gone to his last school 'traumatised' and things had changed from then on. There was no way we could have known; even Nathan himself didn't know.

I sensed that a whole new generation of young men and women were emerging, who had quite a different style to people of my age and background. And when prophetic words like that single out a person, it is likely that God has something special for them. The Bible is full of ordinary people receiving extraordinary words. But of course, the only extraordinary people in the world are those who know that everybody is ordinary— but for the grace of God.

It seemed to me that prophets were often either ignored or stoned—and I didn't want either. I feared that many would resist the Holy Spirit and God's word. I knew it was impossible to resist the Spirit and keep one's sanity, never mind one's church. But sadly, those who say they believe in the Holy Spirit most often seem to be the ones who resist him the most.

I felt called to be a prophet and a visionary. But this was merely a beginning. The seventies and eighties had been demanding but exciting. I sensed that the nineties would make them shadows by comparison.

But while all this was going on, the media were not slow to pick up on new churches and national initiatives. How we are perceived can be as important as what is actually going on. The messenger and the media were important strands woven into a similar period of living out a vision and being prophetic. But not all the media attention was good.

'You even turn the radio on—and you're likely to hear Gerald's voice. I think he's becoming omnipresent!'

Bryn Jones

'The point of having an open mind, like having an open mouth, is to close it on something solid.'

G. K. Chesterton

Chapter 7

The Messenger (1972–1980)

The news is not the news, as Malcolm Muggeridge astutely observed. It is merely an extraction of events taking place at any one time. God is writing his own news, and it is hardly likely to be what we see on our television screens or read in the newspapers.

The first front-page spread in which I was featured was in the *Challenge* newspaper. 'Four hours to live!' shouted the headline. The text continued:

> Unconscious and with multiple injuries after crashing a motor-cycle, Gerald Coates was given four hours to live when he was seventeen. Yet within ten weeks, he was hard at work as a volunteer cook for a boys' camp.

Copies of the newspaper were purchased by churches throughout the United Kingdom in their thousands, and distributed free to homes.

Crusade for World Revival's *Revival* magazine carried an article entitled 'The House Church Revolution', in which I was featured with long hair. I looked like an additional member of Status Quo.

Author Alan Richardson noted, 'In Britain alone, there are now estimated to be in excess of 1,000 prayer groups meeting regularly in private homes and hired halls.' Writing positively about the baptism in the Spirit, church growth and the discipleship in Cobham, he observed, 'Also worthy of mention is the fact that, in the past twelve months, the church has given away over £2,000 in outreach and to other ministries.'

There were only twenty wage-earners in the Cobham Christian Fellowship then, but that pattern of giving was to mark the next twenty years of our development. (£2,000 then would be equivalent to over £10,000 today.)

The Nationwide Festival of Light in 1971 received national publicity, although I was not at the heart of the organisation. However, Peter Hill did ask me to speak at regional rallies.

The *Kent Herald* gave a mixed reaction. 'Two thousand marchers set out to prove that Jesus is alive and well' was the front-page headline. Frances Hant wrote:

> Kingsmead stadium, more used to the roar of a football crowd or the high-pitched scream of speedway machines, was filled with a different noise on Saturday—the united sound of 2,000 voices joined in the expression of one ideal—a love of Jesus. The events which led up to this act of faith began during the afternoon, when Christians of all creeds, ages and races gathered to start a march of witness through Canterbury, crammed with weekend shoppers and traffic. Several drivers were heard to use the name of Jesus, but not quite in the context of the rally!

Photographs of the marchers, the crowd at the stadium, and of a jubilant nun were featured alongside the lengthy article, which continued:

> Mr Gerald Coates, who kept the continuity between the different parts of the rally, often encouraged the audience to give its festival salute, in the form of a raised arm and

hand, rather reminiscent of the salute performed at a different sort of rally just over thirty years ago.

She had obviously not read much of her Bible recently.

Peter Jennings, for the *Church of England Newspaper*, covered a meeting at London's Royal Albert Hall, entitled 'Praise God Together'. It was part of the series which began at the Friends' Meeting House in Euston and grew, entailing a move to Westminster Central Hall. Eventually we concluded the series at the Royal Albert Hall. Most took place in the mid-seventies. Malcolm Muggeridge, Peter Hill, John Noble and I were among the main participants. Peter Jennings reported:

> 'I think that the institutional church is of very negligible importance,' Malcolm Muggeridge told more than 6,000 people who packed the Royal Albert Hall last Monday. 'If I thought that the survival of Christianity and all that it means depends upon institutional churches, then I would be in despair. It is where the institutional church has been most rigorously destroyed and persecuted, namely in communist countries, that the spirit of Christianity burns brightest. One of the great fallacies of our time is to imagine that men can change things. Men are trying to live without God, and they can't.'

In February 1976, the influential *Buzz* magazine, founded by Pete Meadows, interviewed John Noble, Maurice Smith, Mike Pusey and me. In a favourable and objective main feature, Pete wrote:

> What has become known as the House Fellowships Movement has mushroomed over the last few years. The movement has no shortage of critics. To check things out first-hand, I spent four mind-stretching hours with four recognised leaders.

In July 1975 Rod Badams wrote for *Reformation Today* (No. 26) an article on 'The Evangelical Sub-Culture'. It was a scathing attack on anything remotely charismatic.

He called the Festival of Light 'an ambitious, enormous, grandiose nothing'. He spoke of

... folk-heroes who have been given, or have taken, positions of power, authority, prestige and influence among cult followers. In the south of England, Denis Clarke of Worthing, Gerald Coates, Barney Coombs of Basingstoke and Peter Hill, who founded the Festival of Light, are key figures.

Concerning Jimmy and Carol Owens' musical, *Come Together*, he observed:

They combine instant evangelism with unbiblical, thoughtless, and undemanding worship. ... These occasions are clan gatherings along the same lines as pop-festivals.

It was his opinion that 'papers such as the *Evangelical Times* are to be commended for high standards all round'.

The *Evangelical Times* was indeed a well-thought-out and well written publication, but it was completely anti-charismatic, and in my opinion prejudiced, unreasonable, unbiblical and cultish itself.

The *Daily Telegraph* reported:

Meetings of Christians unattached to any church have been attracting more people during the past two years. Numbers have grown from 300 in a London hotel room to 3,000 at Westminster Hall in the spring.

But as time went on, favourable reports in the Christian press gave rise to concerns among Christians in leadership. In 1975, Michael Harper, director of the Fountain Trust, became convinced that people like me would

... attempt to force the church into one mould. ... They neither have Scripture on their side nor history. History does not concern them very much. Gerald Coates writes in *Fullness*, 'The present movement of the Spirit will cause all that is purely cultural, traditional and historical to be discarded.'

Against this, Michael Harper argued that:

The church cannot escape from time and its own historicity. The house church movement itself is cultural, traditional and historical. ... Stay in your churches, but be patient and God will renew them.

I had to say fifteen years later

I don't believe God is renewing denominations. I can hardly think of more than a handful of churches throughout the United Kingdom that have been thoroughly renewed. I can think of many groups that started in empty, derelict or redundant buildings. I can think of some where the original congregation left and the minister started all over again with a new, charismatic, evangelical congregation. But there is not the slightest sign that God is renewing entire denominations, though he is renewing people.

Michael Harper was to become a good, though distant, friend and in later years took positive steps to build bridges with various house church leaders.

Hywell R. Jones also wrote for the *Evangelical Times*. Weighing up the writings of the house church movement, he covered publications by George Tarleton, Nick Butterworth, John Noble, Hugh Thompson and myself. He gave a very fair selection of quotes, scriptures and ideas contained within these booklets—all of which caused no small stir in the early- and mid-seventies. They were privately funded and distributed. Hardly a bookshop would touch them. In his article, Hywell Jones wrote:

How are we to evaluate this approach? We would prefer not to engage in public debate with those who share with us, and are concerned for, a true and powerful testimony of the Lord Jesus Christ today. We would rather confer together in private on those matters which relate to our separate existence and to our common lack of influence on unbelievers.

But they never did get together with us. As a main feature, it was nevertheless a fair article. It concluded:

If a relationship between people is to take such precedence over any doctrinal understanding by them or between them, what will become of the church? Will it continue to be 'the pillar and the ground of truth' as it should be? Or will it not degenerate into the very kind of religious group that these people abominate? And what worth will it be as God's instrument in the world? If 'the King is to be brought back' and set on his rightful throne, then his word must not be sacrificed to his Spirit, nor his Spirit to his word.

Many of the new churches that were to be linked into apostolic teams and networks received good teaching from Scripture in specialist groups, as well as major platforms. The latter also tended to be motivational and prophetic. Many new churches which, for one reason or another, were unable or unwilling to get linked-in, fell foul of the very concerns of Mr Jones.

As Tony Campolo was to say, 'We should always take note of our enemies' (and, I would add, those who may act like our enemies) 'because they are partly right.'

Philip Hill wrote an article in the *Evangelical Magazine of Wales*, in response to my booklet *Not Under Law*. The article contained the following lines:

What is an antinomian? In Christian theology, antinomian means against law. (The law means the whole Law of the Old Testament, in its three parts: civil, ceremonial and moral—the Ten Commandments.) It is an old heresy, occurring in the early church, and corrected by Paul in

Romans 6: 'Shall we ... sin, that grace may abound?'
Antinomians sometimes prefer to be called 'anomian' (no
law). In this way they hope to present a more positive
view of their beliefs.

I was never antinomian in thought, word or deed, and
resisted all attempts to be categorised as such, but Mr
Hill described *Not Under Law* as 'a popularly written
booklet propounding antinomian ideas'. He referred to

> ... [their] unbalanced use of the Holy Spirit and their
> jaundiced view of the Reformation tradition. We will not
> return evil for evil by caricaturing them.

But he went on to do just that:

> *Not Under Law* provides a perfect excuse for libertinism
> and anarchy. If such an attitude continues, it will not
> stand still. It will become a whirlpool of brilliant confusion,
> fascinating and fatal. It would draw into its vortex
> helpless innocents and spew them out as spiritual drift-
> wood.

Philip Hill was the Welsh travelling secretary for the
Universities and Colleges Christian Fellowship (UCCF,
formerly IVF).

Not Under Law sold almost 20,000 copies—a remarkable figure, as most were sent out fröm the home of Pete
and Judy Murray, members of the Cobham Christian
Fellowship. Even as it was going out of print, most
bookshops declined even to order it for customers.

The heart of the booklet was to make up a chapter in
my first paperback, *What on Earth is this Kingdom?*,
published ten years later. Fifteen years after *Not Under
Law* was published, some of the opponents of my 'grace'
message were preaching a similar message and writing
major articles in international periodicals about Law
and grace. Most of it looked as though it had been lifted
from *Not Under Law*. I was pleased.

At the close of 1976, the *Christian Graduate*, published by the UCCF, wrote an editorial around *Not Under Law*, expressing in careful and tender tones their concern that it had gone too far. They avoided inflammatory reaction. It was well written.

The Plymouth Brethren magazine, *The Witness*, in 1977 was also concerned about the house church movement and about Law and grace. One reviewer commented,

> Regrettably, such movements, in seeking to express the freedom of the Spirit, often go to extremes, which makes them even more suspect in the eyes of the establishment.

I didn't mind being suspect 'in the eyes of the establishment'. I had my own suspicions about the establishment, and they were to be confirmed forcibly, on an annual basis, as they lost a million members throughout the seventies and another million in the eighties.

So *Not Under Law* and, later, *Free From Sin*, were to be the platforms upon which I was to be charged with antinomianism on the one hand, and sinless perfectionism on the other! No wonder I felt schizophrenic. Coverage by national Christian papers and magazines only raised people's curiosity—and sales of the booklets.

The fact that the Cobham Christian Fellowship was something quite new in the United Kingdom attracted a great many letters and visitors. So much so, that at some meetings there were more visitors than members.

Realising we were spending too much time with visitors who had no commitment to our goals and values, we went underground. There was no publicity about where or when we met, so that we could build up the community and evangelise the area. Rodney Kingstone, a friend based in Worthing, noted, 'I'd rather catch fresh fish than de-cure the kippers!' The fresh fish were the un-churched.

However, the Cobham Fellowship realised they were

no longer on their own. Groups small and large were springing up all over the country. Some sort of publication was needed. The name of the magazine was *Fullness*. Graham Perrins was its editor and Maurice Smith co-ordinated articles. Nick Butterworth and Mick Inkpen excelled in graphics. It carried no advertising, and only occasionally promoted a worship album, song sheet, book or tape that was highly recommended.

It was mainly read by members of the house churches (later to be called new churches) and also by leaders, because of its well written articles, thought-provoking content and radical ideas. It would not be unusual for authors to receive congratulations ten years after publication ceased for articles we wrote for the magazine.

Despite this growing influence, only one magazine ever did a major profile on any of us during this period—*Crusade Magazine*. The year was 1977. It was reprinted in the *Church of England Newspaper* in 1979. The article was entitled 'The Grit in the Oyster'. Introducing it, editor Derek Williams wrote:

> Gerald Coates, a leading light in the house church movement, has attracted controversy as well as a large following. ... He is a fluent speaker; words roll easily off his tongue. In voice (and build) he is rather like Cliff Richard; thoroughly suburban but with a dash of sharp London lemon rather than Surrey plum. ... Probably the best description of Gerald Coates is that he is a lovable maverick. Get inside his heart and mind, and you find he is not the ogre he has occasionally been made out to be. Maverick he will always be. But there can be no pearl without grit; and where would the oyster be without it?

I rather liked Derek Williams.

Bob Gillman from Romford had written a song which he sang in his fellowship one evening. Within months, it was all over the United Kingdom, and within years, all over the world. 'Bind Us Together' was its title, and in the autumn of 1980, the *Bind Us Together* album and song book preceded a major tour throughout Britain. Songs containing biblical perspectives on worship, praise, relationships and unity were interspersed with narration, Bible readings, dance and drama.

The twelve-city tour finished in London with three presentations at the Royal Albert Hall on January 2nd and 3rd 1981. Hundreds of people became Christians. Others were baptised in the Holy Spirit. Many allowed God to deal with the resentment, bitterness and hurt that cause so much damage in God's family.

Most of the venues were packed to capacity. In Manchester, the doors were closed but the queue of those trying to get in stretched for 100 yards. They returned to the Free Trade Hall several months later. In all, almost 25,000 came to the presentations.

The live events were infinitely better than the album, which was hailed as a new *Come Together* for the eighties. However, it bore few of the qualities, or indeed the anointing, of the recording narrated by Pat Boone ten years previously.

News of the new churches, the publications and *Bind Us Together* reached Sweden and I responded to several invitations to speak at leadership conferences there with my friend John Noble. The national newspaper *Hemmets Van* wrote of these churches, 'Love and care are the foundations.'

While Scandinavian countries were picking up news of house churches in the United Kingdom, controversy continued with a well written series of articles by Colin Duriez in the *Church of England Newspaper*. The six major feature articles raised further interest—and hackles. In one of them, Duriez wrote:

The house church movement poses a challenge which no part of the church—or its many parachurch organisations

—can afford to ignore. What is the main thrust of the Holy Spirit's work today? How can we know this thrust?

The articles were well researched and fair, and asked such perceptive questions as, 'Can the new wine of the house church movement be captured in the wine-skin of words?' He offered the following analysis of the movement:

> Though no one knows the full extent of the house church movement, there are at least seven streams of house churches. The three strongest or most important streams at present seem to be the Harvestime group, based in Bradford; the group of churches centred around Chard; and the circle of churches which includes the genial and public figure of Gerald Coates.

In the fifth article he wrote:

> Gerald Coates is very much a sign of things to come. While thoroughly committed to independence, he has strong links with, and exerts a palpable influence upon, both the charismatic movement and the non-charismatic church.

The series concluded:

> The house churches have changed our way of viewing the church. More and more churches practise a three-tier system—the cell or house group; the local congregations; and inter-church coming together or other inter-church links.

But what had been criticised in the early seventies became acceptable in the early eighties. Institutional churches simply took on board house groups, team leadership, the raising of hands in worship and recently-written songs.

However I lamented, 'They've changed their liturgy, but they've remained the same.' I feared that 'their basic commitment is to their denomination; commitment to the kingdom is secondary. So often they simply go with the flow of what's acceptable.' I believed, quite rightly as it turned out, that in time many would revert to type.

Anyone reasonably secure in their identity is likely to have a few enemies—as well as committed friends. I found I was no exception. Soon there would be articles from journalists devoid of standards. New ground can only be broken once. New ground was being broken, and so was the mould the church had been in for too many decades. Even colleagues would act like enemies. Being a messenger for the living God seemed to me to be a bit like a game of crazy golf in a storm. Life tends to go along a somewhat cryptic and angular course. I was wondering if I would end up identifying with the controversial William Burroughs, who said, 'I like life— but not the one I have.'

Intermission
Photo Gallery

*In the garden,
28 D'Abernon Drive*

*Gerald and Anona on their
wedding day 18 Mar 67*

Gerald and Anona in 1970

157

Paul, Simon and Jonathan Coates

Anona Coates   *Gerald in action at*
                                Sheffield's Octagon Centre

Larry Norman, Malcolm Muggeridge and Gerald at Malcolm's home in the early eighties

With R. T. Kendall

With John Stott in London

With Bonono in a South African township

Boys in South African township with a gift from the Cobham
Fellowship

Gerald in South Africa

Gerald with interpreter Robert Kyanja in Uganda

Gerald in Uganda with the then Minister of Education Joshua Mayanja-Nkangi (now Minister of Economy and Planning)

Sheila Walsh, Gerald and Valeri Barinov on
the day of his arrival in the UK

Gerald, Cliff Richard and Romanian pastor Petru Dugulescu

*David Steel MP with Gerald in the Jubilee Room,
House of Commons, during Jubilee's Valeri Barinov campaign*

John Wimber with Gerald in Surrey, 1990

'Anyone own this boy?'—March for Jesus, Hyde Park

*Gerald, Roger Forster and Laurence Singlehurst outside
Number Ten*

Gerald and Anona with Laurence Singlehurst on the March for Jesus

March for Jesus sets off from the London Embankment

Roger Forster, Gerald and Lynn Green

Gerald with John Noble

Cobham's Leadership Team with Dale and Jean Gentry

'He spoke with a certain what-is-it in his voice, and I could see that, if not actually disgruntled, he was very far from gruntled.'

P. G. Wodehouse

'Are there any cheap humanist jokes? Man only knows.'

Alan Coren

Chapter 8
The Media (1980–1990)

One paper called me 'a cross between Kenneth Williams
and Billy Graham'. A leaflet entitled 'The Charismatic
Conspiracy' referred to me as the one who headed the
'*Fullness* pyramid'! It explained:

> The house church movement itself has a highly organised
> pyramid structure of authority, with ultimate power
> residing at the peak of the pyramid.

My friend John Noble quipped, 'There are no pyramids
in Israel—they are all in Egypt.'

Apparently, the conspiracy involved charismatic
heresy and mixing with Rome; it was likely to be
deceived by Roman Catholicism and its evils. Within a
few years, Stella Bartlett wrote another, similar article
implying that Billy Graham, Mother Theresa, Bob
Mumford and Gerald Coates were taking the new
churches and the charismatic churches into the Roman
Catholic Church!

This astounded me, as I had never been in dialogue
with any leading Roman Catholic about anything
whatever—never mind unity. The only Catholic meeting I
ever spoke at was at London's Westminster Central

169

Hall, when the two and a half thousand people present heard a clear and direct message of salvation by faith alone, which got a standing ovation.

The presentations of The Banquet which Norman Miller and I organised in 1983 and 1984 were attended by about 12,000 people on each occasion. These events introduced the house church brigade to contemporary music and the Greenbelt brigade to praise and worship.

But Greenbelt's *Strait* magazine didn't seem to like what we were doing. Despite The Banquet's size, and quality of speakers and musicians, it barely got a mention. A press release from the Banquet office ended several months of speculation about whether there would be another event. 'The Banquet is on—and that's official,' it was headed. It then detailed the venue—Wembley Arena again—and who would be taking part. Publications that wanted to speak to the organiser out of office hours were also given my ex-directory home number.

Strait's three-line inclusion of the event stated: 'The Banquet—Wembley Arena—it's on—that's official. You'll be getting a press release soon! Phone Cobham 5905—ex-directory!'

To many, it seemed a deliberate attempt to minimise the event and ridicule me. We changed our phone number after that!

A further small article appeared in *Today* magazine (formerly *Crusade*) in 1983, entitled, 'No More Mr Nice Guy'; it stated: 'Gerald Coates declares war on nice, irrelevant Christianity.' Most articles continued on a fair level.

In 1983, *Renewal* magazine interviewed me in a fairly brief 'My Day' series. Whether it was poorly written or whether I majored on minors isn't clear. It did rather give an impression that I sat around drinking coffee, talking to friends, taking my boys to McDonald's and listening to Elton John and Keith Green records. I still had a lot to learn about handling the media. Two other major publishing events received national exposure and reaction which put us in a less than good light.

The first was in the Assemblies of God magazine, *Redemption*, in July of 1986. The editor asked for an interview. We met in London's West End as it was mutually convenient. The issue was to cover the subjects of Christian liberty, law and grace, and rules and freedom in the church. The editor asked penetrating questions. It was in the main a well written article, doing our teachings justice and teasing out difficult areas. By any standards, it was a fairly radical departure from the magazine's norm. For example:

EDITOR: Would you sweep aside all the accepted standards that have grown up over the years; for example, regarding Sundays, alcohol, head coverings etc?

GERALD: By and large, yes. I think the Lord's Day Observance Society is nonsense. The New Testament teaches that the early church met on the first day and every day of the week. For the first three centuries of Christianity, Sunday was a working day, until Constantine was converted. Every day is the Lord's Day. If some people want to keep one day special, that's up to them. Similarly, if I feel that all days are the same, I can mow the lawn on a Sunday, watch TV, go down to the beach—that's fine too! I take the view that the 'hats' issue was related to early Christian culture. The Corinthian women were saying, 'We're free, we don't have to be bound by a culture in which a shaved head was a sign of a prostitute.' Paul was telling them to put their veils back on because of their culture. He was not telling them to wear hats because it was spiritual.

The article was to shatter dearly-held principles of thousands of Assemblies of God readers. It continued:

EDITOR: You do seem, though, to be playing down the authority of the Scriptures over individual believers.

GERALD: We have taught people to be biblical, but to be biblical is to be led by the Spirit, not the Bible. I am not saying we don't need the Bible. Rather, I'm saying that the Law plays no part in the New Covenant. We've been given the Holy Spirit, and the Scriptures tell us to live by the Spirit. The Holy Spirit will honour the Scriptures—Jesus did, and we should do no less than he did. But more than that, the Holy Spirit will lead us into truth, into the study and absorption of Scriptures, into relationship and submission to leaders. The Scriptures never ask us to live scripturally. Rather, they ask us to live by the Spirit. We don't want to do that, because it means taking risks. That's why we like to get as much into black and white as possible—but that doesn't work, either. The Bishop of Durham recites the Thirty-nine Articles with his fingers crossed behind his back!

EDITOR: I'm still intrigued as to the relationship between this 'living from within' and the authority of Scripture. Can you elaborate a little?

GERALD: We know from the Scriptures, especially 1 Corinthians 13, that the 'life from within' is one of love. Love doesn't steal my best friend's wife's affections, diddle Harrods out of their coffee money [the interview was at Harrods], or criticise people we haven't been to privately. Respect for God, for self, and for others is at the heart of love. God's given us the Scriptures to give us an understanding of how he's dealt with nations, individuals and situations. They are a unique piece of literature. When someone comes to faith in our fellowship, we teach them the Scriptures in order to find out what God is like. The new life in the Spirit will always be in harmony with such an understanding.

EDITOR: A unique piece of literature! I think I had better ask you the question I've been skirting around. Do you believe the Scriptures are infallible?

I thought for a while, shrugged my shoulders, shook

my head and said I couldn't come to terms with it. I'd made the classic mistake. I was now talking to the editor, quite simply because he was enthralled by my perspectives and stimulated to ask even further questions, running out of tapes and enjoying the time no end.

Those of us being interviewed should always remember that we are talking to tens of thousands of readers, not to the man with the microphone. I'd ended up sharing a personal reservation. I wasn't an academic; the original manuscripts of the Bible no longer existed, but I did believe in the complete authority of Scripture, and everything I did, personally and in Pioneer-related churches, supported that.

I went on to say, 'I want to emphasise that we do give full authority to Scripture, and all we do is in accordance with the general tenor of Scripture.'

But the editor commented, 'I'm sure we'll have plenty of letters about that!'

They did! Hundreds and hundreds of them. The interview, and my theology, was a talking-point in scores of leadership forums and conferences. The magazine was rumoured to have lost hundreds of subscriptions.

True, the editor had said, 'I could never print that,' and I had responded, 'It would be more than your job's worth'. But without reference to me, they decided to go ahead with an edited version of the interview which I never saw until I spied a copy on a friend's coffee-table.

The Evangelical Alliance General Secretary, Clive Calver, commented, 'This is one of the biggest issues I've had to face since I've been at the EA. Gerald's looked upon as an evangelical leader, his influence far exceeds his authority—and what's more, he's a friend of mine!' Clive protected me well, as did many other Christian leaders—though a few cancelled meetings. I was treated as persona non grata by some for several years.

But I had been foolish. I believed in the full inspiration and authority of Scripture, and should have said so. If I was playing at being controversial, it was a costly decision. If I turned a public interview into a private conversation and thought I could get away with it—I would have to learn the hard way. But failure is not disaster—it is the fear of failure that becomes disastrous.

The second, and infamous, publishing event of the eighties was the 'Andrew Walker affair'. Andrew Walker was warmly disposed to the charismatic movement and decided to write a book. It was entitled *Restoring the Kingdom*. Written from a sociological point of view, it covered the beginnings, personalities, aims and objectives of the house churches. He put the various streams of the house church movement into groupings. Many house church leaders didn't like it, but they had given the denominations a lot of stick. It wouldn't hurt for us to get a taste of our own medicine.

It is true I was always concerned about house church leaders of whom a bad word wouldn't be said inside their circles, and of whom a good word couldn't be heard outside of them! If some platforms were so open and porous that they couldn't hold a conviction between them, the danger of some of the new church platforms was that they were so closed, they couldn't hold a contradiction between them.

The book was published after several interviews between Andrew and myself. It was, to my mind, a fair representation of what the movement was about, and although I didn't share some of his perspectives and conclusions, we promoted it as a well written explanation and history of the new churches.

But the new churches were not just growing, they were changing. Some groupings were becoming a little more closed, though leaders denied that. Others, who had kept themselves to themselves, appeared to be more open. Probably Andrew Walker saw me as a fairly junior partner in the whole set-up. He related more easily to people like David Tomlinson, who had once been with Bryn Jones when based in Middlesbrough but had left Bryn and moved to London.

A new edition of *Restoring the Kingdom* would be needed, to explain and document these changes and developments. Material was updated and added. The book was published. No interviews or phone calls took place between the author and me even though my name had been mentioned in the new material.

Although still a father leader in the Cobham Christian Fellowship, my main work was now with the Pioneer Trust and team. The trustees looked after the financial and legal aspects, and the hand-picked team cared for churches, in a consultancy role or in apostolic partnership. We trained leaders and evangelists, worked with youth and launched or supported initiatives such as the Jubilee Campaign, ACET (AIDS Care Education Training), and the March for Jesus.

Most of my time was spent overseeing these initiatives, acting in an advisory capacity and, now that I was released by Cobham to do so, travelling the nation and overseas. To do this, I was financially supported by eight fellowships I have worked with, one of which was Cobham. All profits on my books went to the Pioneer Trust. Anona tithed regular income into the Trust, and we paid most expenses ourselves, not wanting to draw on Trust funds. My car and most travelling expenses were covered out of my own pocket. My role on the Trust was non-remunerative.

Cobham heard me speak publicly no more than seven or eight times a year, but I met with the elders frequently. They remained my closest friends.

One morning, as I was clearing mail in our office, the

phone rang. It was a Pioneer trustee. The Trust had recently launched the AIDS initiative, which, as an independent agency, would soon care for more dying AIDS patients in their homes than any other independent agency. The Trust also funded Danny Smith of the Jubilee Campaign, and directly or indirectly underwrote some Jubilee projects and trips. March for Jesus had their offices within the Pioneer office block and they were also funded by Pioneer, both financially and with personnel.

If at times I had overestimated my own abilities— which I most certainly had—it seemed that others might have underestimated me.

'Have you seen Andrew Walker's new book?' the trustee asked. I thought I knew what the trustee was referring to.

'Oh yes,' I replied. 'At least, I've not exactly read it, but I have heard about it. But I don't mind, that's Andrew with a little bit of tongue-in-cheek journalism.' There was silence on the end of the phone.

'Well,' he said, 'I think if I were you, I'd not be at all happy about it.' There was another pause. Were we talking about the same thing?

The author had drawn an illustration from *The Wind in the Willows*, likening Dave Tomlinson to Ratty, John Noble to Badger and myself to Toad of Toad Hall. Much worse has been said about me than that! As it turned out, that wasn't the only reference I had not seen. The author had stated that the purchase of our Esher home '. . . led to the accusation of milking funds— from his own followers and those of his fellow-leaders'.

Dave Tomlinson had hosted an event called Festival that drew several thousands together each year. I had been involved in its planning, along with John Noble.

In 1984, we'd taken up an offering, on behalf of the Festival organisers, all of which was handled by Team

Work led by Dave. It was to go to Third World projects. I never handled any of the money, nor indeed saw any of it.

People also contributed jewellery, which Rob Dicken, the Pioneer Trust administrator, endeavoured to sell. Seeking to get good prices, we had hoped to see the collection broken up, though jewellers were keen to buy it as a whole lot. It seemed a girl at Festival thought the offering was too emotional, and that I was milking people's emotions.

Whether the book's charge was over Festival funds (which I had no access to) or Pioneer Trust funds (which as an unpaid director I have no access to either) is not clear. Neither I nor our trustees, team or friends have ever heard of such an accusation from 'followers' or 'leaders'. The author concluded that these charges were not 'altogether well-founded'. It clearly left room to believe that they were true in part, if not 'altogether'. This was unacceptable to trustees and advisers inside and outside of Pioneer.

This was not a personal issue as far as they were concerned. They believed it was unintentional loose wording, as indeed Dr Walker acknowledged. Printing an accusation that a director of the Trust was supposedly milking funds was not going to increase resources for our work in the Pioneer network of churches, training programmes, ACET, Jubilee or March for Jesus. If the press, the Charities Commission or the Inland Revenue were alerted, the results could have been most damaging.

Advisers said, 'This must not become a personal issue between you and the author. The book is in print and thousands have been sold—it's a matter for the publishers.' Our solicitor put it in the hands of a specialist libel solicitor who, having read the offensive passage, agreed I'd been libelled.

The solicitor wrote to the publisher, Hodder and

Stoughton, whose legal department replied with a standard response. The publisher then asked Clive Calver to arbitrate. Pioneer wanted an apology from the author and publisher, the withdrawal and pulping of the books, as well as damages and costs. Author and publisher were willing to send an apology but did not want to destroy the books; instead, they wanted to put an erratum slip inside each copy. They offered to pay legal fees and costs but not damages.

In the event, a compromise was reached. Pioneer dropped their request for damages and Hodder and Stoughton dropped their request for an erratum slip rather than pulping. I received letters of apology from the author and publisher, the books were withdrawn and pulped, and initial legal costs were paid.

I thought that was the end of the matter. It had been a bumpy ride, with the Christian press picking up on the story and nobody benefiting from the publicity. But this was not to be the end.

A personal letter from Andrew Walker to me was apparently sent to the publishers for their initial perspective. It was forwarded to me without comment and so I received it as a letter from the book's author. The letter was shown to two or three key Christian leaders in the evangelical world. It was not a helpful letter.

While speaking at Spring Harvest, I then received a phone call from the BBC saying they had received a press release from the publisher about the whole affair. I was astonished. I had no more thought of sending out a press release giving my version of events than I expected the publishers to. A Christian newspaper editor phoned me to ask what was going on. The conclusion was, they would not be publishing the story at all in the light of the 'tacky' press release. Andrew Brown of the *Independent* newspaper phoned to say that he had been told of the incident and they were going to run a story. Happily, they didn't.

Since then, Andrew Walker has interviewed me for a third publication on the new churches. We shook hands, and it seemed warm and cordial. I do not believe there was any evil intent, but my trustees have a responsibility to our supporters and the authorities. We had to take action for the sake of others.

The regular press outside of Christian publishing are rarely interested in the church unless statements are made by the Archbishop of Canterbury or an infamous bishop. Of course, if you get caught with your trousers down, like Jimmy Bakker or Jimmy Swaggart, that's a different story.

Apparently, not only should adultery, wife-swapping, fornication, homosexuality and promiscuity be expected in society, but Christian leaders should also simply regard such behaviour as normal. However, if Christian leaders do those things themselves, they can expect immediate international stardom. Very few in the United Kingdom had ever heard of Bakker or Swaggart before their disgrace.

On the one hand, the press totally disregard institutional Christianity as being of no value and on the other, ridicule it relentlessly. When a viable alternative came along they didn't know how to handle it. On the BBC Two *Friday Report*, I was interviewed by Michael Delahay.

'You evangelicals are all into show business, aren't you?' he warmly enquired.

'I'm not sure what you mean,' came the reply.

'Well—your whole approach is American, more like show business, isn't it?'

I smiled and asked, 'Have you been down to your local church on a Sunday recently? Grown men dress up in long gowns, carry around handbags that emit smoke, bow down to trestle tables covered in coloured cloths and light candles either end—we couldn't possibly compete with that!' The reaction was edited out, but Michael Delahay nearly fell off his chair with laughter.

'I've never seen it like that before,' he said. They all laughed.

'You see, we wear regular clothes,' I continued. 'What we do is normal. Obviously, the psychology of leading and communicating with ten people in someone's front-room is quite different to communicating to 10,000 at the NEC in Birmingham, which we've just done. But what we are doing is normal. What I've just described to you, about historic church life, is where there is show business!'

I wrote to Michael Delahay thanking him for the sympathetic treatment we received. Michael Delahay replied with a correction. He pointed out that he hadn't given me sympathetic treatment, but rather objective treatment, which was our right.

David Coombs, from BBC Radio Four's *Sunday* programme, asked if I would contribute to their national radio programme dealing with the subject of Hallowe'en. An Anglican philosopher and a witch were to be the other guests. 'I'm not sure I'd get up at 6 am for an Anglican philosopher,' I laughed, 'but for a witch—I do like a challenge!'

After breakfast at Broadcasting House in Langham Place, the Anglican philosopher turned to me and requested, 'Please don't tell listeners I'm a member of the General Synod, will you?' It was the last thing he should have told me!

The show went on the air and after general news, the interviewer was taken-up with the novelty of having a witch on the programme. Spells and formulas, demons and darkness were explored. She was a warm-hearted somewhat naive spell-caster. Her hairstyle looked as though her stylist had drunk a bottle of whisky and gone prematurely blind.

The interviewer then turned to the Anglican philosopher. 'What do you think of all this?' she said. He explained that sin was found in structures in society, that there were no such things as demons and all this was a lot of nonsense.

I reacted in uproarious laughter. 'Well, it's a real shame you weren't around when Jesus was here. He went round casting out demons—and you could have told him he was wasting his time because they don't exist! You should be ashamed of yourself—you a member of the General Synod as well!' The crew on the other side of the glass roared with laughter and shook their heads.

Brian Deer from the *Sunday Telegraph* visited one of our meetings and interviewed me. A series of March for Jesus events had recently coincided with an event promoting the Church of England's Faith in the City initiative; in this, a bishop and an actress had gone up in a balloon.

In his article, Brian Deer observed, 'Baptists, Pentecostalists, house church worshippers, and other fundamentalist Christians upstaged the Anglican balloon with a string of huge public events.'

I was reported as saying, 'People are withdrawing their support from dying church hierarchies and placing their faith in living networks.'

Brian Deer continued: 'Publicly, the Anglican bishops welcome the interest that evangelicals spread.' However, he also reported private opinions of a more caustic nature. For example, one said, 'These sort of charismatic, excitable churches are good for the young, but people don't stay in them. My family call them *Dallas* people, because they have such lovely teeth.'

The journalist concluded, 'The March for Jesus

organisers will be more than happy that they prompt thoughts of *Dallas*, while Anglicans look like *Brookside*!'

I didn't do so well with the 1989 *Mail on Sunday* colour supplement magazine, *You*. 'Gerry and the Peacemakers' was its title. Val Hennessy wrote the article. 'We'd like to do a piece on the new churches—we've been told they are the most exciting thing happening on the religious scene in Britain today,' she explained. She attended a prayer meeting at Tolworth Recreation Centre with about 1,000 others. Prayer and praise, news and teaching filled the one and a half hours.

'It was wonderful,' she said to Anona. 'All those young people! How do you do it?' She then took me out for lunch. I gave her my message on ACET, Jubilee, inner city church-planting projects, March for Jesus and various anecdotes I thought would make a good story. She pursued the Cliff Richard friendship with questions relating to where he lived, the price of his house, how much he earned, what he was worth—most of which I avoided, pleading ignorance.

When the article came out, Anona couldn't believe it had been written by the same lady who had come to the meeting and taken me out to lunch. It said:

> Forty-five-year-old Coates, short legs, low-slung bum, freshly blow-dried hair and oleaginous smile, clapped his hands and shimmied up on the platform beside the band. Hallelujah! Ignore the basketball nets and the giant Milk for All poster, and he looked like the compère of *Sale of the Century* ... You can picture Coates, Anona and Cliff, all washed in the blood of the Lamb, sipping Perrier by Cliff's pool and rapping sincerely about theology, homosexuals, the starving, joining hands and maybe singing a few bars of 'Let the Flame Burn Brighter'.

There was not a paragraph about all our Third World initiatives, church-planting projects, training plans or work overseas. We had been set up, and we had walked straight into it. She was probably tipped off by someone with a grudge. Somewhat defensively I reacted, 'Well, Jesus got set up—and he saved the world.' But the article was somewhat of a shock, a genuine disappointment, and made me more careful about future press opportunities.

Nigel Lloyd, Managing Director of the *Mail on Sunday*, admitted they'd had almost fifty letters, all of complaint. These were quite unsolicited. Indeed, I had asked the church in Cobham, and other churches, not to write en bloc as it wouldn't look good or do any good. But Mr Lloyd thought it was a very fair piece of journalism about a 'worthy' section of church life.

Writer Stan Gebler Davis later declared that he would rather be interviewed by the KGB than by Val Hennessy. Journalist Maria Harding called her

> ... a Fleet Street doyenne, whose offbeat exposés of the famous and infamous have now been collected for posterity in book form. The prospect of being given the once-over by Hennessy has been enough to throw strong men into a fit of the vapours.

Unfortunately, these insights did not hit my desk until several months after the *Mail on Sunday* printed the article.

I still receive occasional letters, wildly hostile, full of scriptures, mostly vitriolic. Virtually all are unsigned and nearly all begin 'I'm writing this to you in love'. I am always glad they are not enemies! But few have had either the courage, insight or common sense to address their concerns openly to the person they were concerned about.

One Christian leader in the Assemblies of God denomination circulated a story that I was seen with 'a crate of whisky' in my chalet at Spring Harvest. Two or three churches refused to promote or attend Stuart Bell's Grapevine event in Lincoln because of that. No one bothered to check with us. When Stuart asked if I had taken a crate of whisky to Spring Harvest, I replied, 'Have you ever been to Skegness in March?' But joking aside, the truth was I hadn't. Not a crate, a bottle or even a miniature of whisky, or anything else like it.

It seemed I was nearly always in trouble for something I'd said or done, or, as was usual, something I was supposed to have said or done. Certain Christian leaders are so dull, boring and predictable that nobody ever expects anything to be said or done apart from what traditional tram-lines determine. I was wanting to find new ways of saying biblical things, just as my master did 2,000 years ago.

Jesus often did not use Scripture, but clearly stated what was true. He used illustration, parable and humour, so I tried to do the same. In gifting, I am prophetic, not a Bible teacher, and I could never work out why people expected me to expound the Scriptures, word by word, line by line. There is little room in conservative evangelicalism for intuitive gifting. Having silenced the prophets and then the women—or was it the other way around?—it left an extremely cerebral approach in pulpits for decades.

But to me, wildfire is still better than no fire.

Although I preferred speaking to writing (words came more easily from the voice than from the pen), throughout the eighties I wrote hundreds of thousands of words. My plea is for an orthodox, biblical, vibrant faith. This was echoed in a series I did for the *Church of England Newspaper*. It continued in the *Christian Herald*; in a contribution to a book compiled by Tony Jasper; in the nationwide March for Jesus magazine, *Forward*; and in Graham Kendrick's magazine/newsletter *Make Way*.

Apart from these articles for magazines and newspapers, I also wrote under a pseudonym.

Bread magazine, then edited by Peter Sanderson for the Elim movement, was looking for writers. But they were not looking for Gerald Coates. Someone refused to have my articles published. But Peter was keen to get me to write. A series appeared under the name of Simon Jon-Paul, the names of our three sons! No one apart from Peter discovered who the real author was.

I was interviewed for *21CC*, *Restoration* magazine, and in 1989, the *Jesus Army* magazine. The July 1990 *Renewal* magazine carried a warm profile written by Ian Boston and edited by the courteous Edward England.

Previously, throughout the eighties, I felt I had to write myself. Putting words beside one another and trying to make sense of them was not something I found altogether easy. In 1983, *What on Earth is this Kingdom?* was published, sold out and was reprinted within the first twelve months. In the book, I put the talk 'Pioneers and Settlers' into chapter form, listing the differences between the two.

Settlers I typified as being 'double-minded, afraid of making mistakes, continually stifled, their concerns are seldom translated into actions'. Then I explained that settlers thought that 'eternal life is to be safeguarded and truth defended', whereas pioneers thought 'eternal life is to be enjoyed, explored and truth released'.

The settlers' 'concept of God was a perfect gentleman who never raises his voice, never interrupts plans already made (always agrees with and submits to the notice-board), has a number of attributes some of which are better than others'! Pioneers had 'no static concept of God, having only a living relationship. God is seen as gracious but not British, in the habit of interrupting plans made in his name that he has little or nothing to do with.'

I finished the list by saying that settlers thought 'sin is breaking with tradition and failing to observe cultural etiquette', whereas pioneers thought 'sin is doing anything that makes God unhappy'.

Other chapters were entitled: 'A Kingdom Without Rules (Law or Grace?)'; 'A Kingdom Free From Sin'; 'Friends! Friends! Friends!'; and one that the many independent house churches who were not to survive should have read: 'Eight Reasons Why Fellowships Level Off Or Collapse'! The final chapter, entitled 'My Mediocre Recommendations . . .' included

> Strip all clergy and denominational leaders of ecclesiastical status and let those with God's gift get on and do what they have to do . . . Separate church and state. Agnostics and atheists influence the so-called running of the church. And close all denominational headquarters overnight . . . Tragically, even some of those who sound like eagles, on closer inspection live like parrots.

In 1984, a series of essays was put together, some satirical, others humorous and a few, serious. Put into book form, it was entitled *Gerald Quotes*. My friend Kevin Allan supplied me with various things I'd said, or was supposed to have said. It was reprinted with what I thought was an awful cover in 1988. Outpost Trading (Pioneer) have the only stocks left.

Essays were entitled 'If the joy of our Lord is our strength, it's little wonder that the church in Britain has been so weak and ineffective'. Digging at unreality, I wrote, 'Most Christians are nicer than God himself.' Trying to get rid of the theology that 'lays it at the foot of the cross', I wrote, 'Your ministry's probably what you like doing.' With personal experience, one chapter was entitled 'I sometimes think it will take a major surgical operation to get a generous heart into evangelicalism'! Both were published by Kingsway.

It was Hodder and Stoughton who asked me to write a slim paperback in the 'Foundations' series. Entitled *He Gives Us Signs*, it was published in 1987; there were only moderate sales and Outpost Trading (Pioneer) hold the remaining stock. The book dealt with prayer, miracles, signs and wonders.

Also in 1987, Kingsway published *Divided We Stand*. Chapter headings included: 'The House Church Movement—is it the house of God?'; 'The Church of England—has the roof caved in?'; 'How free is the Free Church?'. Controversial chapters were entitled: 'The Cross—the central point of Christianity?'; 'Apostles—disturbing, divisive or incredibly important?'. Going back to familiar ground, I also wrote on 'Holiness—back to Victoria or on to victory?'

These books, along with *Not Under Law*, published in the early seventies, and republished by Good Reading, and the subsequent *That You May Not Sin* (reprinted as *Free From Sin*) have sold about 100,000 copies, mainly in the UK.

Strangely enough, I became well-known for something someone else had written about me. The infamous Adrian Plass, as an anagram of my name, had come up with 'God's ale crate'. I was greeted every few weeks with that. I preferred what the students of St John's Anglican College had come up with: 'Rages at old CE'; or, as another had found, 'God's later ace'!

I also had the dubious honour of being the only person mentioned in David Taylor's *The Book of Cobham* who was actually alive!

In the spring of 1990, Barry Norman hosted a series of interviews around the theme of values in a changing, shifting society. I was asked if I would submit myself to an interview with Barry Norman on issues relating to the liberty of the press, censorship and pornography. My opponent would be Martin Scorsese, the director of the controversial film *The Last Temptation of Christ*. I realised it could be confrontational, so took advice and went ahead, praying that good would come out of it.

On my arrival at Broadcasting House in Langham Place, the researcher told me, 'I hope you won't be disappointed, but Martin Scorsese has had to fly to America for a funeral. Will you be OK with Barry Norman for half an hour on your own?' I was, and the interview came out OK, despite a heavy cold.

Ian Cotton, a freelance journalist who worked for the colour supplement of the national *Sunday Times*, showed up at the 1990 Spring Harvest. He had seen our programme on BBC 2's *The Friday Report*.

Partly because he lived at Farnham and Cobham was so near, he decided to make Cobham and our ministry a focal point from which he would be able to write about the broad work, beliefs and goals of the evangelicals.

It was in the main a most constructive article. It included the journalist going up to London with one of the Cobham teams who work with the homeless. He visited small and large meetings in and around Cobham, and interviewed many people. To say he was thorough was an underestimation. The prestigious article reflected his attention to detail, and our work was treated generously and objectively.

TVS (Television South) came to the Cobham Christian Fellowship and filmed Petru Dugulescu, who was a key leader in the Opera Square demonstration in Timasoara, Romania. It was also broadcast nationally in May 1990. It was most objective. Several weeks later, an arsonist destroyed a local warehouse which the Pioneer Trust and the Cobham Fellowship were using to store tons of literature, food, clothes, toys and medical supplies for a trip to Romania's orphanages. BBC's Television South

East, and Radio's County Sound and Mercury, covered the story. A dozen local papers made it their top feature. Thousands of pounds in donations ensured the trip took place. They also enabled stocks of literature to be reprinted.

Sometimes it seemed the so-called secular media was taking more interest in the work of evangelical new churches than the Christian press. I enjoy the media, but, in the words of Pete Meadows and Clive Calver, I had to 'learn how to handle them'. But one thing I rarely speak about to the media, secular or Christian, is my ministry to individuals. But it has been another significant strand woven into this twenty-year period. For way back in 1970, God had given me aspirations to influence the influential.

'I've grown up confused—Elton John and Cliff Richard have been my role models.'

Jonathan Coates, eleven years

'Success covers a multitude of blunders.'

George Bernard Shaw

Chapter 9

The Pastor? (1973–1990)

I always found it somewhat inapt that the quite remarkable writer, speaker and prophet, A. W. Tozer, should be called a pastor. In the fifties, prophets were barely recognised in Tozer's Chicago. You were either an evangelist, a Bible teacher or a pastor. So often, I shook my head in bewilderment that anybody could fail to see that Tozer was a prophet.

As for myself, considerable mail was inappropriately addressed to 'Pastor Gerald Coates'. Sometimes it was even 'Reverend' and, on one occasion, 'Bishop'! As I walked through Cobham one day, a postman shouted out, 'Congratulations on your promotion!' Whatever else I was, I hardly fitted the traditional role of pastor. But in small ways, I became a friend of a few influential people and, in some cases, a pastoral adviser.

One day, shopping in Cobham High Street for some stationery, I visited Farrant's. A tall stand with stationery on one side and greetings cards on the other stood in the centre of the shop. As I moved along, a man was moving parallel on the other side. Both of us reached the end of the stand together, I with pad and envelopes in hand, and he with a clutch of greetings cards in his.

We saw each other and looked surprised. We knew each other but couldn't work out how! One of those absurd conversations started immediately.

'Good morning, nice to see you again!' I exclaimed.

'Good to see you,' the man replied. 'I've not seen you for ages. What are you doing now?'

My mind raced. Slowly, it was coming together. When I had gone to Fetcham Primary School as a little boy, I'd seen this man walking his dog. Then, when I went to work at Epsom, the same man visited the building on Saturdays.

Thinking out loud, I replied, not answering the question, 'I remember as a little boy seeing you walking your dog when I was going to Fetcham School. Then I used to see you at Epsom, at H. L. Reid on the crossroads.'

The man looked nervous. 'But I've not seen you there for a long time—are you still in Epsom?'

What should I say? If I said I was leading a fellowship, the man wouldn't know what I was talking about. I wasn't a clergyman and I didn't like the word 'pastor'. I wasn't a trained minister. But Billy Graham had been around in the United Kingdom; he might remember him. 'Well, I left Epsom to become an evangelist, you know, like Billy Graham.'

Suddenly, the man threw back his head and guffawed with laughter. It wasn't a smile, a supercilious grunt or anything like that. This was full-blooded, outrageous laughter. The entire shop froze. The people serving behind the counter knew me. Some had been at school with me. At the top of his voice, the man shouted, 'Oh no! You've not been converted by this bloke Gerald Coates, have you?'

A strange thought went through my mind. What would Laurence Olivier do in this situation? I paused. 'Well actually,'—I paused again—'I am Gerald Coates.' The poor man nearly had a coronary on the spot.

But our influence, often based on half-true rumours and completely true stories, was spreading. It was still the mid-seventies. I was to speak at Truro Cathedral, invited by Don Double, a brave evangelist who visited many places in the United Kingdom and overseas that other evangelists wouldn't even give a thought to.

At the close of the meeting, a man came up to me. 'Excuse me, but are you the Gerald Coates who lives in Cobham?'

I knew by the concerned look that I was not about to be congratulated for my talk. 'Yes, I am.'

The man shuffled around as he stood by a large Norman pillar. 'Please forgive me for asking this, but I've heard it now from two or three sources. Is it true you dress up in a purple robe and call yourself the Bishop of Cobham?' I nearly spat my teeth out. But that wasn't all. He went on, 'And is it true that you wear a silver cross around your neck?'

Most stories and rumours have a grain of truth in them. I did have a purple polo neck sweater and, in the late-sixties, did occasionally wear a stainless steel cross. These stories kept me happy for days on end.

To a limited degree my prayers to be influential were being answered—but this was not quite what I had in mind!

I had met Lord Longford on the Trafalgar Square plinth, during the Festival of Light. I never met him again. Malcolm Muggeridge I watched on television many times. We met in person, also in Trafalgar Square. Peter Hill took Anona and me to meet Malcolm and Kitty with two or three of the London brothers. Malcolm was really keen to meet Peter after the Trafalgar Square rally, and subsequent meetings, and agreed to Peter's request that we join him. Malcolm and Kitty were surrounded by farms. They lived in Sussex.

Anona had brought Paul and Simon, who were around four and two years old. Kitty went to a drawer and pulled out one or two toys. An aeroplane was given to Simon. Before we left, he'd broken it beyond repair. But, interestingly enough, Simon had sat on the quarry-tiled floor listening intently to Malcolm, clearly not under-standing a word he was saying, but nevertheless en-thralled. Children are sensitive to atmosphere and Simon clearly liked this atmosphere.

Shortly after that, there was the Royal Albert Hall interview. It was quite a coup to get Malcolm Muggeridge not only at an evangelical meeting (he'd shunned most church meetings), but at a charismatic house church major event such as this. During the course of the interview, Malcolm told the 5,000 people present:

> One of the great fallacies of our time is to imagine that men can change things. A simple example of what I mean is the incessant use of the word 'problem'. If you are old, as I am, people say you have an aging problem. If you are a boozer, they say you have a drink problem. The misuse of the word is that it assumes that every single situation in which we find ourselves has an answer in men. It hasn't. In fact, precisely what is wrong with the world is not an energy crisis, or an inflation crisis, or any of these things. What is wrong with the world is one very simple thing: men are trying to live without God, and they can't! ...
>
> There is a crisis in what we call western civilisation. Western civilisation is collapsing. The situation as I see it is rather as it was when the Roman Empire—which seemed so enormously strong, which was so fantastically rich, the centre of everything—collapsed. I think of Augustine in Carthage, as a messenger told him, 'Rome has been burnt.' To Augustine, this meant the end of everything he believed in. Then he reacted as a Christian, as we must react, and he said to his folks: 'Men build cities and build civilisations, and men destroy cities and civilisations, but the word of God has been revealed to human beings, and especially to us. That cannot be destroyed.' In a sense, it would be a terrible thing if this crisis was not upon us. The most appalling thing that could afflict mankind would be for it to be possible for men to live as they are now trying to live. They cannot—

and hence the crisis. We know that these great upsets of the world cost dearly in human suffering, and that is a terrible thing. But we also know that God is not mocked. It will be a dreadful thing if western man's lifestyle was viable.

Peter Hill asked, 'What do you think about the role the institutional church has played in the past? Do you think it has had any impact?'

John Noble interrupted, 'You mean the establishment?' Muggeridge replied with a glowing smile:

I think it is like NATO, or all of these other different fantasies that human beings create. One of the strange things about men, when their way of life is collapsing, is they create fantasies to believe in. They believe in NATO, they believe in something called a social contract. All these are pure fantasy, they don't exist. I think the institutional church is of very negligible importance. However, if you said to me, when I was a young journalist in the USSR in 1932, that it would be possible for Christianity to thrive, after all the attacks of the régime on every sort of transcendental view of life, attacks supported by the whole power of the state, I would have said this was madness. But this is what has happened . . . I know that everything in newspapers and on television is lies. Nobody could possibly know that better than I do. But still, you read them and you listen and you get a picture of a totally corrupt, decadent world. And then one comes to a gathering like this, and it is wonderfully heartening. The Holy Spirit is enormously active and I'm quite sure that out of this great crisis will come a new light. But exactly how, in exactly what circumstances, exactly what suffering is going to have to be undergone, that we cannot know.

I knew I wasn't a pastor, even though most of my time was spent caring for people and teaching in the growing Cobham Fellowship. I would also spend a lot of time writing to people in response to requests for help and advice. But the meeting with Malcolm and Kitty influenced me to influence others.

On one occasion we visited the Muggeridges to find Andrew Boyle present. Malcolm was cutting logs while Kitty went to make some tea. There was a nervous and embarrassing silence. I didn't much like the silence. 'Tell me about yourself,' I requested nervously.

'Nothing much to say, really.' This was the man whose voice could be heard every lunch-time on Radio Four saying, 'This is *The World at One* with Andrew Boyle.' But he was also a journalist.

Malcolm had been in MI6 during the war. Andrew was intrigued by the 'fourth man' in the Burgess, Maclean and Philby affair. So he wrote *Climate for Treason*. 'I told him not to get involved in it,' Malcolm told me. 'It's a messy business.' Messy it was. He was threatened, he found out more than he could ever print, but Anthony Blunt was uncovered.

It was some twelve months later that we returned to Robertsbridge to find Andrew there again. 'Well, what a coincidence,' I remarked to Malcolm.

'Oh, I'm afraid the book has taken its toll, as I told him it would. He's been most unwell, spying's a nasty business. You'll find a link between spying and homo-sexuality. The whole spy network is an old boys' network mainly consisting of homosexuals.'

Several years later, American rock singer Larry Norman asked me if he could meet Malcolm. We travelled together, to find Malcolm and Kitty with two Roman Catholic nuns, a mother superior from Venice and a young slip of a thing who'd been in India. Malcolm was fascinated by India and so was Larry. The talk was blending well. I was pleased. Large cups of tea and Kitty's famous fruit-cake were gratefully enjoyed.

As the afternoon drew to a close, Malcolm turned to Larry, whose long blond hair fascinated Kitty no end. 'You're a singer—sing us a song.' It was the sort of request that couldn't be declined. I was embarrassed. This could be awful. No band, no lights and no PA.

Larry cleared his throat and the five of us sat back. 'Make me a servant,' Larry sang, somewhat out of tune and with a croaky voice. Suddenly, the room was filled with the Holy Spirit. When Larry had finished, everybody sat in silence; not a word was spoken. It was difficult to break into the atmosphere.

Eventually I coughed and shifted in my seat. 'Malcolm, thank you for having us—we mustn't outstay our welcome.' We said our good-byes and I drove Larry to the High Street in Robertsbridge.

'Well, that will be one of the holy moments of my life,' Larry murmured.

Larry came to stay once or twice after that while on tour. He would sit in the bedroom reading the boys' comics much of the time, but generously purchased a range of *Star Wars* figures for Jonathan.

Jack Parnell was a prolific songwriter and a good drummer. He was best known for leading the orchestra years previously on *Sunday Night at the London Palladium*. His car's collision with a motor-cyclist was reported on front pages of the national press. He was sent to prison.

While there, he reflected on his life. I grew tired of the gossip and badmouthing that was going on about Jack, often by people whose problems seemed worse than his. I wrote to Jack to assure him of my prayers. Jack replied, 'Thank you for your prayers, Gerald. I've been praying as well—and it looks as though they've been answered.' The prison chaplain had helped him find faith.

Jack was involved for a while at the Arts Centre Group in London with Nigel Goodwin, where he met a number of Christian artists. One Christmas morning, the phone rang. It was Jack. 'Happy Christmas, Gerald,' he said, warmly and sincerely. It was the only call we received that Christmas Day.

It was several days later that I reflected on the call. Was it Jack phoning a few friends to wish them well, not being a great letter writer or sender of cards? Was there more to it? I had always been challenged by Anglican prayers confessing sins of omission. Non-Anglican evangelicals majored on the sins of commission, asking forgiveness for those things that had been done that shouldn't have been done. But I was impressed by the Anglican understanding of sins of omission. Should I have been more sensitive to Jack on Christmas Day? Had I omitted to have him round to our home? Was I being oversensitive?

But living life without Christ for so many years, along with the pressures of show business, had taken its toll. Jack moved away to East Anglia and into retirement. But his faith moved with him. In 1990 he played at Greenbelt.

Norman worked at Threshold, the Moody Blues' record shop in Cobham High Street. One day he phoned me and asked, 'Would you meet me for lunch with a girl-friend?' A red Mercedes sports car, complete with an extremely attractive, slightly-built woman, arrived on time. We went to Cobham's La Capana, one of the finest restaurants in the area. There were difficulties; could I help? She was Marietta, wife of Status Quo singer Rick Parfitt.

We visited on several occasions, meeting members of the group, were guests of the Parfitts at a Quo concert at Wembley Arena, and Anona and Marietta met for lunch regularly.

One afternoon, the phone rang at 52 Between Streets. Uncontrollable sobbing was heard at the other end. Heidi, their two-year-old daughter, had fallen into the pool and drowned. 'This is the longest journey of my life,' I commented to Anona as we drove fifteen miles to the village south of Guildford.

We had had to miss the funeral as we were in the USA. But the Parfitts had also been introduced to the Arts Centre Group. Nigel Goodwin had become a friend and adviser, and they found help from one or two other Christians. Rick went to Greenbelt with Cliff Richard and played in his band. Sometime before the funeral, Rick and I sat on the floor of Rick and Marrietta's beautiful home, reading 1 Corinthians 13 and praying together.

But it was all too much for Rick and the marriage broke up. Marietta became good friends with Cliff Richard and his Christian friend and manager, Bill Latham. Rumours of 'more than friendship' were unfounded.

Evangelist Eric Delve had put me in touch with Dave Markee, who at the time was bass guitarist with Eric Clapton's band. We occasionally met for lunch and fellowship. Dave had a friend in Detroit who had met John Lodge from the Moody Blues. John lived in Cobham.

A discussion over a Detroit dinner about Christianity led to one of the table saying he was an evangelical. Up piped John, 'An evangelical—so am I.' John was a charming man who lived in a beautiful home. His attractive wife, Kirsten, could have been an interior designer. John came to one or two meetings and invited Anona and me for supper with some of his friends. John and Kirsten asked me to give thanks for the meal and we talked about the Christian faith for most of the evening.

Before some of the London brothers went their separate ways, they arranged a meeting in London's Trafalgar Square. The date was set. We then received a letter from the Commissioner of Police, asking us to reconsider. Could we find another date? The reason was simple. The National Front and the communists were marching on that day, and would meet as they passed through Trafalgar Square! All police leave had been cancelled and 2,000 men were on stand-by. 'I like a challenge,' I quipped—so we went ahead.

In excess of 5,000 people assembled in the square to worship, pray for the nation and thank God for the new and good things that were happening in the land. A piece of paper was slipped to us. I announced that 'on the left', the communists would be coming through and 'on the right', the National Front would as well. We sang and worshipped as two thin blue lines came in from two opposite corners of the square. Behind them were communist marchers on the one side and National Front marchers on the other. Small fights broke out, and the language was rich.

We asked those assembled in the square to kneel. 'They're dissatisfied with the government,' I explained, 'but there's a kingdom, a government in the earth which isn't like any human government. Let's pray they'll find the King and his kingdom.' I led them in a sung version of the Lord's Prayer. Then all 5,000 sang in tongues, quite spontaneously. It was a remarkable moment. On-lookers watched in astonishment. The event was attended by several key evangelical leaders, who were both moved and influenced by what they saw.

Another meeting was at nearby Buckingham Palace. A girl who worked for the Royal Family, and continued to work for them for many more years, invited me to supper to talk and to pray with staff members. Her Majesty the Queen was just a few rooms along, having her own supper. Expectations were that the meetings would continue—but they didn't.

It was to be many years before I found out that the girl who gave the invitation married one of the staff. It was not a happy marriage. She eventually left Buckingham Palace to work elsewhere for the Royal Family.

She turned up to meet me in Kent years later and introduced herself. 'I feel I've let you down,' she told me. 'I always felt that out of those who came to speak, you should have been the one who went through the Buck House doors on a regular basis.' But it was not where my influence was to be.

The lady in question still works for the Royal Family. But there was not a shadow of disappointment in my heart when I heard of these missed opportunities, due to her personal and domestic misfortunes. I had now come to learn that no one and nothing in heaven, hell or on the earth can thwart God's plan for a life. But I did believe I could disqualify myself from reaching the full potential God intended. Samson's soft spot for the ladies disqualified him almost for ever. Joseph's sense of being special and therefore superior caused many wasted years.

Oh yes, I knew that in the end they, and many others like them in Bible times, found their way back to God and did great things in his name. But I would often ask, 'What if Samson had not allowed Delilah to seduce him and to cut his hair? What if Joseph had not shared his secret with his brothers? What would God have accomplished through them in their time?'

As for the Royal Family—who knows? Many fine Christians, including John Stott, Dr Billy Graham and a host of lesser known individuals, have been an influence on members of the Royal Family. It doesn't matter who's doing the influencing, providing it is there.

However, after the AIDS initiative, ACET, had been running for a little over a year, royal contact was made. The Chairman, Sir John Ford, who had once been Britain's ambassador to the United Nations had a meeting with the private secretary of a member of the Royal Family. A message came back to Dr Patrick Dixon, conveying a good measure of approval and indeed, congratulations, for the AIDS initiative.

Members of the Royal Family and entertainer Cliff Richard had lent support to various AIDS initiatives. Almost all such organisations were in fact pro-gay. Some were positively promoting homosexuality as a lifestyle, through literature which could only be described as pornographic. At last here was an AIDS initiative which gave unconditional care to dying AIDS patients while upholding biblical and moral values. There would be several internationally known personalities who felt more comfortable with this particular initiative.

So far it seemed I was the one being influenced by the influential. My own influence on them was either limited or barely recognisable.

And then there was the dear old C of E (well, old anyway). The longer I was in full-time ministry, the more disenchanted and annoyed I became with Anglicanism.

The house churches, and particularly some of their leaders, were to exercise and influence people and groups way beyond their normal jurisdiction. Not only were they the fastest growing network of churches and Christians in the United Kingdom, but they were to influence major sections of denominational Christianity with their theology, non-religious style, music and worship songs.

Running parallel to this growing influence were, increasingly, babbling, befuddled bishops, many of whom agreed on everything (other than orthodox Christianity) because, it seemed, they believed in nothing. Bishops were the face of British Christianity but most did not reflect its changing heart.

On one occasion, several years into full-time ministry, but still living by faith, I thumbed a lift into London. I was to speak at Westminster Central Hall that evening. This temporary chauffeur took me to within half a mile or so of Westminster. I thanked the driver, who continued on his way to his next business call. I continued my journey on foot.

As I stepped off the pavement, a large black limousine brushed my jacket. The shock was immediate. Had I stepped off one second before, I would have been mown down by the Daimler. I didn't see the chauffeur but did see the passenger. It was the Archbishop of Canterbury!

On the front cover of one Anglican magazine was a priest with a plate of bread and a chalice of wine. 'The most important thing in the ministry is to offer the sacraments,' it stated. I roared with laughter. I am not remotely sacramental in that sense. I have come to the conclusion that even Jesus could have had no idea how people would twist those words 'as often as you do this do it in remembrance of me'. This was in the context of a meal, it was with friends, with meat and herbs.

I was also angry about the arrogance of certain Anglican leaders who, despite losing hundreds of thousands of members while I'd been in full-time ministry, felt they should be centre-stage. They might as well come to terms with the fact that the also-rans, the nonconformists, were moving centre-stage theologically, numerically and influentially. I often quip, 'The Church of England is the only denomination to have more members in their churchyards than in their church buildings.'

And yet I purposely made many friends within the Anglican church. The Evangelical Alliance hosted a day for several hundred leaders. John Stott and I were the two speakers. But it was a bad day all round, with appalling weather. Trains and buses were cancelled due to snow. Hundreds of conferees sat in the Friends' Meeting House in Euston in desperate need of a cup of coffee, rather than two talks on the kingdom of God! But John Stott graciously invited me to a day at the London Institute of Contemporary Studies, which was much more successful. We also enjoyed one or two private meetings.

Later Dr Billy Graham and Cliff Richard took part in a London leaders' event. Anona and I were on the platform. John Stott came in on the other side. I went to greet him, not being sure if I would be remembered. John looked up, smiled and declared, 'My dear boy, give me one of those charismatic hugs!' We received many letters stating that our embrace was one of the best things of the evening!

Later, he wrote to me saying he thought Dr Patrick Dixon's book *The Truth About AIDS* was excellent and that he would be including material from it in his updated version of *Issues Facing Christians Today*.

Despite my anger at some of the bishops, and at the lack of discipline over theological reprobates and clergy, who seemed to me more committed to the Church of England than they were to God, I responded to invitations to speak in evangelical Anglican churches.

Peter Sertin was Vicar at St Michael's in Paris. Anona and I spoke at the church and at a special conference in which several made a positive commitment to Christ and were baptised in the Holy Spirit. When Peter returned to the United Kingdom due to bad health, he took up work in nearby Guildford but we never saw each other during that period. In fact the only contact was when Alvin Stardust stopped to help a lady whose car had broken down. They lived in the same area. Having lived in Paris for several years, she had no idea who he was, took him home to meet her husband and it turned out that her husband was Peter Sertin. Peter then moved to Camford Magna, near Dorchester.

Noel Richards and I took part in an interdenominational event, Pentecost Praise. That night we touched the hem of revival. The meeting finished at 8.30 pm. Then the Spirit fell. Fourteen-year-old boys and adults were weeping and repenting without any human contact.

Another important Anglican connection was in Knightsbridge where the modest Sandy Millar led Holy Trinity Brompton, and was the main initiator in a church-planting strategem in South West London. Sandy and I developed a warm and growing friendship which was reflected in Sandy's involvement with the March for Jesus, and he represented us publicly on several occasions. He is a kingdom man first and an Anglican second.

On one of my rare Sunday mornings at home, I wandered through the lounge where Jonathan was flicking channels. What appeared to be a lively evangelical charismatic service was being broadcast. What was this? Jonathan grudgingly gave up his cartoon film for his dad. There was not a clue as to which group this service represented. They were singing new church songs, there were words of knowledge and prayers for the sick. Worshippers raised their hands in the air and there was some excellent teaching by the leader.

It didn't have a Baptist feel and it certainly wasn't Methodist. It could be one of the new churches I'd never heard of, but I thought it was unlikely. When the credits went up they said 'St Peter and St Paul, Swanley, Kent'! An Anglican Church! Thrilled with what I'd seen, I wrote to the vicar, David Betts, congratulating him on the content of his talk, the style of the service and the vitality of the worship. Several months later I was endeavouring to make a point at Spring Harvest. The point was that the moment we write people off tends to be the moment when God writes them on!

David Jenkins, the Bishop of Durham, had just come out with some more outlandish nonsense, so I had been particularly verbal with regard to liberal Anglicanism. I then went on to tell the television story, which was of course against myself. I beefed up the story of the church with its worship and teaching, and the fact that I'd watched the entire thing from beginning to end wondering what on earth it was. When I announced it was an Anglican church, the audience loved every minute of it, and laughed and clapped.

At the close of the meeting, attended by almost 1,000 people, a man came up and introduced himself. He seemed vaguely familiar. 'You don't remember me?' he asked. 'I'm David Betts of St Peter and St Paul in Swanley, Kent!' After that, Noel and I were invited back on several occasions for teaching, prayer and leadership forums.

So here I was, slowly becoming one of the public figures in the new church movement, and at times apparently merciless in my criticism of denominational Christianity in general and Anglicanism in particular. And yet God was helping us to nurture relationships with evangelical Anglicans and their churches. At times I thought I was performing an ecclesiastical high-wire act! One slip could be dangerous.

But I was being myself. Matthew Arnold had lived in Cobham between 1873 and 1888 at Pains Hill Cottage. The poet, critic, philosopher and school-inspector was the son of Dr Thomas Arnold of Rugby School, immortalised in *Tom Brown's Schooldays* by Thomas Hughes. He once wrote, 'Resolve to be thyself, and know that he who finds himself loses his misery.' I was being myself despite the high-wire act—and there wasn't too much misery.

The Coates family was about to move just five minutes away from Cobham to Esher. We went to view a specific house. As we walked in, I exclaimed, 'This is a Christmas house.' It was 1985 and from then on, every Christmas-time, there would be a party for around seventy friends. It was possible that this particular mix of people would not be in the same room again for at least another year—for some, never again. It wasn't possible to have the same people every year, as the Coates and Millers had more than seventy friends between them!

Regulars included Clive and Ruth Calver (Clive had his fortieth birthday party there at Ruth's request), Roger and Faith Forster, John and Christine Noble, Terry and Wendy Virgo, David and Enid Pawson, Lyndon and Celia Bowring, Ishmael and his wife Irene, Noel and Trish Richards, Mike and Katey Morris, Roger and Maggie Ellis, Pete and Nikki Gilbert, and Pete and Rosemary Meadows.

Owing to their commitments, some were unable to come every year and some not at all at that time of the year. These included Brian Macwhinney MP and his wife, David and Lizzy Alton, songwriters Trott and Sweet, Alvin Stardust, Nigel and Gilly Goodwin, Ravi and Mrs Zacharius, Rob Frost, John and Hazel Barr and Ray and Nancie Goudie. Adding more colour and panache was Cliff Richard accompanied by Bill Latham.

Cliff and I had first met in a hotel dining-room, queuing for food at a post-Royal Albert Hall buffet reception. Neither of us were participants, but regular concerts were held each January and the 'complimentary' guest list was a bit of a *Who's Who*. As we shuffled toward the table, Cliff discovered his co-traveller lived just down the road. We talked of shops and traffic.

Shortly afterwards, Cliff responded to an invitation to sing and then be interviewed at a marquee which was packed with over 2,000 people, on Cobham's Leg of Mutton site. It was part of our Kingdom Life series of meetings. Sheila Walsh and her husband Norman Miller were about to move in with Anona and me. They were friends with Cliff in their own right. Sheila worked with Cliff both in the United Kingdom and overseas, and it was clear there was mutual admiration.

Christmas was a special time in our household. I was home for almost two weeks, for a start. Cliff liked Christmas as well. So occasionally, we spent Christmas eve singing carols with Cliff and other friends, standing around the Bluthner piano at our Esher home. Mulled wine and the latest stories made them most pleasant evenings.

One New Year's eve, Cliff invited about ten friends to a London restaurant. It got to midnight. The restaurant was packed with the wealthy. A spirit of comradeship and almost of fellowship pervaded the atmosphere. 'What shall we do?' Cliff mouthed to me, tapping his watch as midnight approached.

I raised my wine-glass and stood. 'Ladies and gentlemen, to the King and his kingdom.'

Cliff's guests raised their glasses 'to the King and his kingdom'. Suddenly, all around the restaurant people were raising their glasses, smiling, laughing and toasting the King and his kingdom!

Occasionally, needy folk found their way to Cliff's private house. Invariably, his answer was, 'I can't see you now—you ought to see a friend of mine, Gerald Coates.' Thanks Cliff!

The relationship was mutually nurtured through the work of a team in Cobham who took on the task of replying to the letters which came to Cliff requesting advice and counsel. As a leader of the Cobham Christian Fellowship, Stuart Lindsell oversees this team. Sometimes they handle twenty letters a week. People from various parts of the world, some from nations Cliff has never visited, write to say they have become Christians because of his lifestyle, a few words he said on television, or as a result of going to a concert. Some subsequently went on to hear someone like Billy Graham and gave their lives to Christ.

At the close of Cliff's 'Wembley Event' which drew over 140,000 people over two nights, he wept. I was in Uganda while the concerts were on, but when I returned, Cliff told me, 'I couldn't get over the fact that all these people had come to celebrate my thirty years in show business. But then I do ask at times, "What am I doing?" I meant it when I said at Wembley, "Nothing I sing or say will change your life or affect you drastically." But I was so glad I could say, "There is a God in heaven who loves you. He has a Son, Jesus."'

On one occasion, he was on his back. He has a well-known recurring back problem. Norman and Sheila said, 'Why not get someone to pray with you?' My friend Ian Andrews and I went up to Cliff's and prayed with him. There was an immediate improvement. Having been on his back for many days, he was playing tennis within the next few. The problem is still there but it has not affected him like that since the prayer-time.

In the late eighties Cliff moved from a house on St George's Hill Estate to another nearby area. I confess I was rather pleased when a van-load of plants and shrubs we had sent up to Cliff's in gratitude for various things that Cliff had done for us were dug up and moved to the new garden.

In so far as he could be part of a church, Cliff became associated with the Cobham Christian Fellowship. But he could not be a part to the same extent as others, for obvious reasons. One was his continual international travel. But he came along on occasion when he could. He remains grateful for their prayers, and especially for the group that takes care of those who write requesting literature, counsel and help.

On one of the occasions when Cliff shared in the worship and teaching of the church, I was speaking. The smallish hall was packed to capacity. There were no seats left. Cliff, when he came, always arrived at the last minute. He didn't want to be the centre of attention and, as far as was possible, wanted to worship as everybody else.

On this particular occasion he arrived just as the meeting was starting. He joined in the worship and the prayers. When it was time to sit down, he perched himself on the corner of one of several tables that had been pushed to the side of the hall, creating extra temporary seating. I am in the habit of asking folk to join hands and pray before I speak. At the close of the message, I asked folk to join hands and pray again. To me, touch is important, and the theme of my talk had to do with relationships and friendships.

Cliff and a few friends came back to our house for some light supper. The phone rang and I answered it.

'I thought you'd like to hear this one.' The voice on the end of the phone was relishing what was to come next. 'We brought along a friend, not a Christian, and he hasn't been to any of our meetings before. On the way home I asked him what he thought of it.' The caller paused. 'Do you want to hear the rest?' he asked, laughing.

As it turned out, the young man had disliked the meeting, the music and the speaker! The visitor finished his survey of the evening by concluding, 'And then, I had to join hands with this naff Cliff Richard look-alike!' Apparently he had refused Cliff's hand, and folded his arms in defiance. His wife never forgave him!

David Alton, a Liverpool MP, was well-known for his Pro-Life campaign and nationally televised speeches.

David was one of the first MPs to involve himself in Danny Smith's 'Siberian Seven' campaign. He launched the Jubilee Campaign in the House of Commons with Danny and me. Some of the work David did for the Jubilee Campaign was less widely known. This included visiting Valeri Barinov in Leningrad before his release. He took frequent trips to other parts of Eastern Europe where Christians were suffering for their faith. He became a spokesman for believers suffering for their faith in Nepal, South Africa and other places.

Danny and his wife Joan, along with Anona and me, were invited to David's wedding to the diminutive and attractive Lizzy. It was there I met Cyril Smith, who used precisely the same text in the wedding as I was going to use in my talk at Cobham on the Sunday. We exchanged notes, a handshake and a laugh.

David had put several ideas and projects to me on the occasions when we met in the Strangers' Dining Room, or in his office in Westminster Palace. One or two seemed absurd, but, as the years unfolded, became distinct possibilities.

On one occasion we were talking about the great

divide in Northern Ireland between Catholics and Pro-
testants. I explained how every major meeting I did in
Belfast was picketed. I waxed eloquent about the
Northern Ireland spirit of contentiousness, Ian Paisley
and Roman Catholicism. David drank his soup and
nodded. When he looked up, he nearly swallowed his
spoon. Ian Paisley had come for lunch and had sat at the
next table. His chair was three inches behind mine!

I didn't meet Ian Paisley. But that very week, Mr
Paisley phoned Cobham church leader David Taylor to
offer help to Romanian pastor Petru Dugulescu, who
needed a visa for Germany. He was charming, courteous
and co-operative.

If there was pastoral care, it was not expressed mainly
to national and international names in the worlds of
politics and show business; in fact, in those areas I felt
something of a failure. Despite several finding faith, it was
too late to save some of their marriages. Expressing care
for the famous was not always a simple affair. Anyone in
the public eye is uncertain as to why people show interest.
What is their motive? To take too little interest could
convey a lack of genuine care. Showing too much can be
suffocating. Confidentiality (apart from fairly commenting
on public incidents) is vital for an outgoing relationship.

No—my main pastoral cares were for key people in
Cobham and other Pioneer leaders in various parts of
the country. All are becoming influential personalities.

Through prayer and fellowship I have endeavoured to
encourage and care for Martin Scott who led the Cobham
Christian Fellowship from the mid-eighties. Martin eventually began to oversee a number of churches in the South
and West of the London area, one of Pioneer's regional
teams. Martin put a lot of theological content into my
intuitive responses to issues. Despite the different starting point, there was remarkable harmony between us.

Stuart Lindsell, now leader of the Cobham Christian

Fellowship, and I enjoy an easy relationship. The tension between prophets and teachers known in some churches seemed not to apply perhaps due to our mutual appreciation and need of one another. The same is true of full-time leader Nigel Day, elder and practising solicitor David Taylor, and of local leaders Linda Harding, Derek Williams and Les Coveney.

Black Ugandan Anthony Kazozi had heard me speak at the George Cadbury Hall in Birmingham. A new job was taking him to Kingston in Surrey.

At the end of the meeting he spoke to me. 'My name is Anthony, and I am moving to Kingston. We wondered if you knew a church there that we could go to.'

My reply surprised him. 'Actually, you're not very far from Cobham—why don't you come along and see us?' The young man didn't seem too keen. Without thinking, I turned to him and said, 'I'd like to pray with you. I just know we're going to be working together.'

What Anthony Kazozi thought of that isn't clear. What was clear was that he eventually moved to Cobham and married the attractive, white Tanya, an intuitive girl who probably heard more from the Lord than she thought. Anthony became successful in business, and received several promotions.

When the possibility of a Tear Fund/ACET partnership emerged, working back into Uganda to help AIDS sufferers, I told Patrick Dixon, 'Anthony is your man!'

It was not any easy decision. Going to a Third World country on one's own is one thing; taking a wife and young child into a different culture is another.

Anthony and Tanya asked for advice on a number of issues. After a lot of heart-searching, prayer and not a few tears they returned to my office and told me, 'We've looked back at several prophecies we have been given over the years, including a number from outside of the Cobham area. In the light of your feelings, our own aspirations and these prophecies, we've decided that we'll head up the AIDS initiative in Uganda.'

When the BBC's World Service asked me to host a service for international broadcast, I asked Anthony to read the Scriptures. Anthony's father was still living in Uganda. One day, as he was lying on his bed in his home just outside of Kampala, he turned the radio on. He tuned into the World Service, having not one idea or clue about the Cobham broadcast. As soon as he had tuned in, he heard his son's voice reading from one of the Gospels.

Noel Richards and I have travelled on national and international trips for almost eight years. Much of Noel's work in schools and colleges, concerts and worship seminars, does not involve me. Much of my work in the office, and with leaders and even public events, does not involve Noel. But Noel and Trish have become close friends of Anona and me. We have occasionally holidayed together. We enjoy being in each other's company.

My influence on Noel has mainly been functional rather than personal. Whenever the Richards had difficulties and needed counsel and advice, they would normally go to another couple. I had come to the conclusion that one of the major reasons for friendships splitting up was because the senior person held privileged information about the others. It sometimes made those others feel uncomfortable. How would the information be used? I was keen that we shouldn't involve ourselves too much in the Richards' family affairs, and that kept things relatively simple.

On one occasion, Noel was taking part in another World Service broadcast. I interviewed Danny Smith, and Noel sang a song dedicated to Valeri Barinov, 'One of our Brothers is Missing'. Several months later, a Singapore businessman arrived at the Cobham Christian Fellowship on a Sunday evening and told the following story.

I was driving through Singapore, and tuned to the World Service. I heard this song, 'One of our Brothers is Missing'. It was so moving I had to pull over onto the hard shoulder, and I wept. Several weeks later I had to take my daugher to the Yehudi Menuhin School. My daughter is an accomplished musician, but is in need of further training. The school is just outside of Cobham. As I drove back to the airport, I drove through Cobham and wondered if this was the same Cobham I had heard of on the radio.

He parked his car and stood on the pavement in the High Street. He stopped a man who he thought might be able to help him. He had heard this service. It was lively singing. There was a song about someone who is missing. Was there such a church in Cobham? Little did he know that the man he was speaking to was Stuart Lindsell, one of the leaders!

God had given Noel and myself something to do with our friendship which seemed, albeit in limited ways, to have a growing influence.

Many show-business people, politicians and even church leaders, become cynical to survive. The demands on their time, continual public scrutiny and untrue if not unfair things printed about them, foster that cynicism. Operating in faith in a sometimes cynical environment is a little like walking on water. Although there are no rules for walking on water, my faith in God's ability to get his will done was growing. 'Chance' meetings with personalities in other nations were not unusual.

Adrian Hawkes from Finsbury Park, North London, was on my team. Adrian was a pastor down to his tiny toes, had planted several churches and initiated schools and a college with Christian principles at their heart. At one of the Pioneer team-days, Adrian asked me to meet a church leader from Sri Lanka. He led a church of around 1,000 people and had planted out several others that were large and influential. The pastor had a son whose name was Paul.

I sensed we should pray for Paul and I began to prophesy over him. 'God has his hand upon your life; you feel different to others because you are different. Stay close to your father, for your influence will far outstrip his. God has saved your life on two, no three, specific occasions. There is a purpose for this.' After giving the prophecy, I left Adrian and went back into the team meeting.

Upon Adrian's return, he smiled and asked if we would like to hear a story. It turned out that Paul's life had been saved precisely three times. On the first, soldiers came and beat the family, but went next-door shooting and killing the entire family. Why they didn't kill the Sri Lankan church leader's family is still a mystery. One the second occasion, the entire family were kidnapped and taken to the woods to be shot. The Sri Lankan church leader asked to see the leading terrorist. It turned out he had been in the church leader's Sunday School. They received an apology and were released immediately! On the third occasion, Paul was cycling along with a friend when there was a massive explosion; his friend was killed and a large chunk of metal came flying through the air. If he hadn't ducked he would have been decapitated.

But despite local influence and international concerns, my main burden remained for the United Kingdom. Stuart Bell told me, 'Jean Darnall and you have been the two major influences in my life.' Stuart leads the Ground Level team, which is based in Lincoln and extends from the Humber to the Wash and beyond. I have been a frequent speaker at the Grapevine event, alongside David Pawson, Roger Forster, Ian Andrews, Jean Darnall and Ishmael.

Kevin Allan leads Pioneer Solent and oversees a

group of churches that look to him for advice and care. Roger Ellis leads Pioneer South, another group of churches within the Pioneer network. Both make important contributions to the work of Pioneer. They are men of integrity, openness and honesty.

Steve Lowton in Leeds is another who has looked to us for help, care and advice. Steve leads a growing church on the edge of the city. He sensed the need of relationships at peer-level that were not purely functional.

In the summer of 1990, Steve joined the Pioneer team, which at that time consisted of Rob Dicken, who has administered the team and its affairs for almost ten years; Amanda Collins, who deals with the mail, diary and some of our personal affairs; Kevin Allan, Stuart Bell and Roger Ellis; Adrian Hawkes in North London; and the well-known evangelist Pete Gilbert. Steve Clifford heads up the TIE Teams (Training in Evangelism) and is a senior adviser to the team.

Peter Sanderson shares responsibilities in the South and West of London area and edits the *Pioneer Bulletin*. Noel Richards has created several music forums both for experienced and for up-and-coming musicians, and fronts most of the large Pioneer worship events.

Martin Scott heads up Pioneer South and West of London, and Mike Morris, who works at the Evangelical Alliance as the Social and Overseas Director, became Policy Adviser. Ishmael leads the Glorie Company, a vital ministry to families. Meeting with us also is Dr Patrick Dixon of ACET.

Each of these is a personality in his own right and some have grown into national and international significance. I am a generalist, but I have surrounded myself with specialists.

However, there is no way I could take responsibility for the lives of peer-level leaders across the new churches. Within the new churches there are different theologies relating to apostolic ministry, women in leadership, and the Second Coming of Christ. But divided armies don't win battles. Marks of the new church constituency bear more similarities than is obvious to those within the movement. To those outside the new churches, they all look the same!

So I gathered a group of men together for fellowship, prayer and a mutual interest in one another's ministries. There were also plans to ask new church leaders to a conference I arranged at Sheffield University's Octagon Centre. Each of these men was a personality in his own right and some had significant influence.

They included Stuart Bell, Derek Brown, Barney Coombs, Dave Day, Peter Fenwick, Roger Forster, David Matthews, Phil Mohabir, Mike Morris, Tony Morton, John Noble, Graham Perrins, Dave Tomlinson and Terry Virgo. Others joined us, including Chris Bowater, Nick Cuthbert, Roger Ellis, Faith Forster, Ray and Nancie Goudie, Christine Noble, Noel Richards and Martin Scott.

It was September 1988 when 1,000 new church leaders gathered to consider themes of unity, prayer and fellowship. The initial meetings were for the sharing of information, projects and prayer for one another. After eighteen months we began to work through an agenda which Terry Virgo had supplied. We discussed and studied issues of prophecy, women in leadership, new church distinctives and models for evangelism.

In March 1990, almost 1,000 new church leaders gathered again at the Octagon Centre on Sheffield University campus. If the first conference had majored on the themes of friendship, relationships and the unity which Jesus prayed for as recorded in John 17, this conference had more teeth to it. The main emphasis of the weekend was on evangelism, faith, spiritual warfare and the Apostles' doctrine. The seminar programme dealt with multi-racial issues, social action, prayer and church-planting.

But as I have already said, new ground can only be broken once. A great deal of ground has been broken over the last twenty years. New churches within the networks overseen by teams number almost 1,000. There are at least that many new churches that are not related to any team whatever. In 1970, there were barely any new churches and by 1990, I estimate, around 2,000.

Initially, people in the new churches were drawn from the historic churches, either because they were disillusioned or because they were thrown out. But they were not thrown out because of doctrinal heresy, sexual immorality or anything of that nature. They were thrown out because they wanted to be filled with the Holy Spirit! The institutional church has always been first to persecute a fresh move of God's Spirit.

Numbers in the new churches are always difficult to quantify. 2,000 churches with an average membership of 100 adds up to 200,000. Some new churches remain quite small, perhaps no more than forty or fifty people. But the majority are growing, and several number almost 1,000. Roger and Faith Forster's Ichthus Fellowship in South East London is well over 1,000 strong.

The new churches are moving centre-stage, and remain the fastest-growing wing of the church. They have been criticised for having no social action and being interested only in singing, praying and being spiritual. This is no longer true. They are now involved in overseas initiatives, church-planting in inner cities, work among young people and the elderly, and initiatives in the worlds of education, AIDS sufferers, the suffering church and entertainment.

But the desire of the new churches to move forward, while keeping open relationships with those in evangelical denominational Christianity, makes life a little awkward. Ensuring an extra level of awkwardness was an apparently innocuous attempt at getting the praise and prayer of Christians out onto the streets. These harmless bits of fun gave denominational church leaders plenty of room for anxiety.

Some felt we in the new churches had done rather well in twenty years. But there was to be no premature canonisation! Criticism and suspicion were still to abound. Perhaps there was a level of naivety in me. I had imagined that all evangelical Christians had the same goal: to re-evangelise the nation, to be good news and to share good news. It all seemed so simple. Does it matter who does the job, providing the job gets done? Apparently, it does!

My teaching began to focus on such topics as the relational unity of God's people, as taught in John 17, and strategic plans for reaching the nations with the gospel, in accordance with Matthew 24:14. Where people and people-groups live in unity, there God 'commands blessing' (Ps 133:3). That blessing is so to fill us up that we cannot contain God and his word and so that he breaks out to bless our area, our people and our nation.

When the nations have been networked with the gospel, 'then the end will come' (Mt 24:14 NIV). We should all want to bring an end to the corrupt systems which exist in almost every nation.

Non-evangelical or anti-charismatic religious people do not share this understanding of God and his purposes. But thank God they are diminishing in number all over Europe. The devil picks them off and their blurred message is no longer attractive. They remind me of a flock of ducks I once heard about. Trained to fly repeatedly over a shooting-area, they did so until not one was left. You don't have to be David Bellamy to know that this breed is doomed!

The issue is: what will survive?

'Let the flame burn brighter
In the heart of the darkness
Turning night to glorious day.'

Graham Kendrick

'You are the world's light—it is impossible to hide
a town built on the top of a hill. Men do not light
a lamp and put it under a bucket. They put it on a
lampstand, and it gives light to everybody in the
house. Let your light shine like that in the sight of
men. Let them see the good things you do and
praise your father in heaven.'

Matthew 5: 15–16 (PHILLIPS)

Chapter 10
The Torch-Bearers

The days of boyhood innocence and teenage tensions were over. Aspirations had become achievements, but new aspirations were on their way. The desire to pioneer was enriched by vital friendships and experience. Media encounters continued, and the desire to be prophetic to both public and individual personalities grew. I longed for us to be a light in Europe's darkness.

If the seventies and eighties were decades that promoted progress, the nineties would be a decade emphasising survival. 'Green' issues would dominate international high-level discussions. The church would try to be 'green'.

Denominational Christianity lost a million members in the seventies and around another million in the eighties. Much of the church had seemed to lose its distinctive message. Present a clear message, and people can respond one way or the other. Convey a blurred message, and no one knows what you're conveying. Whatever liberal Christianity was conveying—and it was, all over British television screens—it was presiding over the demise of Christendom as it had been known. But while institutional Christendom was diminishing, the body of Christ was rising up. The Intelligent Fire was answering the prayers of old and young. There was a worldwide interest in the Christian faith. Political and geographical boundaries were changing, many through the prayers and the lives of those who had been lit by this Intelligent Fire.

Despite the demise of institutional faith, a living faith was emerging. 'We are called to be torch-bearers not pall-bearers,' I would often encourage myself.

On occasion, church leaders would ask Pioneer team members for advice for their denomination, churches and future strategy. Many denominational leaders are simply hostages of hesitation. Most are run by administrators, not prophets and evangelists. The best many can do is hope they can maintain the present number and quality of churches. Being asked to give advice to certain liberal church leaders, is a little like advising the captain of the *Titanic* after his ship had hit the iceberg.

I was asking myself some questions. Has the church got its back to the future? Was the Decade of Evangelism the yawning of a new era? We know that no great idea has ever survived unless it is embodied in a group of people. In what way could the ideas of God and history be embodied in God's people today?

I confess I often laugh at liberal church leaders and churches. Laughter destroys fears. It is better to laugh at them than fear them. They have been influential in television's 'God slot'. Semi-intellectual programme participants have included Don Cupitt, John Habgood and David Jenkins. If one claims to be a born-again evangelical, and have any faith in Scripture, it is assumed he has kissed his brains good-bye. National radio is a little different, and local radio certainly gives more opportunity for evangelicals and new church leaders.

At times I have been good at cursing the darkness,

particularly the darkness emerging out of certain institutional churches. But we have also made definite attempts at developing friendships and working with those in the institutional churches whose lights are shining. But I know it is insufficient to curse the darkness, ridicule the theologically banal and castigate errant bishops. A new light must emerge. I believe it is emerging. Its centre is everywhere.

Roger Forster, Lynn Green and I had been friends for many years. Roger's Bible studies in Cobham when I was a teenager had caused a distant respect to become warm friendship. We may not have seen much of each other, but whenever we did it was like picking up the relationship as though we had only seen each other yesterday. Roger had developed from being a travelling preacher to planting churches, creating evangelistic teams, putting theological content into much charismatic activity and had become a spokesman for much new church theology and philosophy.

Lynn Green's origins were completely different. He was Director of Youth With A Mission in England (and later in Europe, the Middle East and Africa). His main concern was evangelism. He and I would meet for lunch once or twice a year throughout the late seventies. Lynn was concerned that the new churches could end up only attracting disillusioned institutional church members. Where was the evangelism? He knew that if they were to make an impact, they would have to become thoroughly evangelistic. His concern was that they might change their liturgy but remain the same. My concern was that the Director and his YWAMers would simply hatch eggs but have no nests to put them in. They would be picked off at every opportunity.

But all three of us developed quite separately and matured with a growing respect for each other.

Up to this point, John Noble had been one of the

major influences on my life. His distilled wisdom has saved me from many relational lock-up situations, and has been a great help in smoothing out some of my somewhat abrasive, reactionary responses in certain situations. The relationship remained good and firm.

Another influence was Dave Tomlinson. Dave had moved from Middlesbrough to inner-city Brixton. Dave wanted to break the white, middle class mentality within evangelicalism. John, Dave and I had been the main initiators of the annual Festival event. It ran for several years in the eighties and attracted thousands of people. While the relationship between Dave and myself remained firm, when Festival finished, it seemed there was little for us actually to do together.

Into that vacuum stepped Roger Forster and Lynn Green. It was unintentional, but proved vital.

Graham Kendrick had written *Make Way*. The music was geared for outdoor marches. Ichthus Christian Fellowship, based in South East London, had gone on several relatively small marches involving their own people.

The early church had no buildings of their own for almost 300 years. They met in homes or the open air. Much of Jesus' ministry including all the major gatherings was in homes or the open air.

It was a developing strategem which went alongside a developing theology. When God linked Roger and Graham with Lynn and myself, things began to accelerate. But most of the best things, we stumble upon quite accidentally. We look back and realise that God must have been in these things. Not through plans, personalities or numbers; things bring honour and glory to God when performed by the Spirit. God himself was at work in a special way here, without us realising it!

Roger, Lynn and I met on several occasions to pray about taking the praise and prayers of the charismatic movement out onto the streets. The small, localised Make Way events had been good strategic manoeuvres. Ichthus had marched through Soho, once a beautiful village, but now drenched in sex shops and all that goes with them. Shortly after their prayers and praises out on the streets, when they gave roses to the prostitutes and offered to pray with the victims of the seedy area, police moved in and closed down all but a few of the sex shops. Residents were delighted. The pimps were less than delighted. God was getting his will done.

So we, the triumvirate, drew Graham Kendrick in to write a script and create a programme for the larger event, March for Jesus. Eventually, Steve Clifford became the chairman of the steering committee, which was made up of senior members of Ichthus, Pioneer and YWAM.

In May 1987 5,000 people were expected to turn up at Smithfield market in the City of London. It had been a place where the saints had been martyred. It seemed a good place for evangelical Christians in the Greater London area to gather and pray. An attractive programme was printed, with songs and prayers containing the philosophy of the March for Jesus.

On the day, as Noel Richards and I drove into the City of London, it was pouring with rain. It was torrential. Would anybody turn up? There was no entrance fee. No ticket to buy. There was no model to follow.

When we arrived, the stage was covered in transparent polythene sheeting. Microphones and equipment were in danger of being damaged. A somewhat dejected group of Christian leaders had gathered. It included members of the Council of Reference (which was drawn from a broad evangelical spectrum). A small but growing crowd were gathering in front of the platform. What we didn't know was that a much larger crowd were being kept under massive arches that were closed off—to keep them from the effects of the rain and to create an orderly event. Perhaps things would be better than they looked. Even a fairly large crowd in the open air looked small. Most people overestimate numbers in closed buildings and hopelessly underestimate them in the open air.

Then, almost without warning, the stewards gave the OK for the marchers who were being kept under the arches to make their way to the front of the stage. Within two or three minutes the front and sides were filled. And they kept coming, and coming, and coming. Despite the torrential rain, by the time we started, police estimates reckon there were 15–16,000 people assembled at Smithfield. Police estimates are always conservative and it is not unreasonable to reckon that there were almost 20,000 people gathered on the day. We sang, and prayed for the City. We prayed against the foolishness of trusting in riches.

As were recounted many times, major events followed, affecting not only the City of London but the whole of the United Kingdom and other parts of the world. What became known as the 'Guinness affair', the insider trading deals being discovered, and then the Stock Exchange crash, all took place within six months. Coincidence?

It was now the summer of 1987. There were no plans to do another March for Jesus. Ichthus were involved in a local evangelistic initiative and ideas were underway for a major London event. Lynn Green's responsibilities were growing into Europe and beyond. But I felt uneasy. We had been caught up in something bigger than we could have orchestrated. Was this God? The Intelligent Fire? Was he lighting a flame that was to be bigger than any of us on our own, or indeed all of us together, could handle?

Anona and I had a number of small meetings and

private engagements in Los Angeles. Roger Forster and his wife Faith had meetings on the other side of LA at precisely the same time. Their son Chris was also working there. We decided to meet up for supper one night.

In the course of the evening I said, 'Roger, I know you have plans to do something local next year and Lynn Green is up to his eyes in evangelistic initiatives. But I'm not sure we ought to leave March for Jesus in the City. Why don't we take it on into Westminster, surely the most influential place in the United Kingdom?'

Roger, a strong-minded leader with deep theological convictions, nodded. But it didn't seem hopeful. Roger and his entire network were geared up to something else. It didn't include the continuation of March for Jesus.

A few weeks later we met again. Roger had spoken to his leaders. They had agreed: they would march in Westminster. This time we prayed about the weather!

On the day, the London Embankment dual carriage-way, from Waterloo Bridge to Hungerford Bridge, was closed. Initially, the police had refused permission for the march. The police had been under attack because of the growing number of events that gave rise to violence and damage. They were uneasy. Pioneer, Ichthus and YWAM networks went to prayer. The next meeting with the Metropolitan Police was completely different. They had done a 180 degree turn around. They couldn't have been more co-operative.

It was not a media event. We had barely sent out any press releases to the Christian press. It had all been by word of mouth, leaflets through our address lists and contacts, and promotion through our own limited circu-lation of in-house magazines. The national press were informed the week of the event and there were BBC and ITV interviews. The national press turned out to a small press conference.

The triumvirate then walked to the Embankment. It was jammed solid with marchers, not only from the Greater London area, but from many parts of the United Kingdom. The event had caught the imagination of evangelical churches almost everywhere, it seemed.

Twenty minutes before the event began, the police sent a message through to the platform party. The Embankment, from Waterloo to Hungerford Bridges, was now filled on both carriageways with praying, singing marchers. Waterloo Bridge still had singing, banner-waving believers streaming across it like ants. The City had been brought to a standstill.

A programme consisting of songs, prayers and a declaration by the triumvirate, Graham Kendrick and Noel Richards, went according to plan. By the time we set off for Hyde Park, the police estimated that there were at least 55,000 gathered.

We sang and prayed our way through Westminster. Roger, Laurence Singlehurst (Director of YWAM UK) and I went down Whitehall to 10 Downing Street. We handed in a letter assuring the Prime Minister of the prayers of evangelical Christians—even though many were certainly not Conservative in their politics. We urged her to care for the sick, poor, unemployed and those marginalised by society. We also assured her that if she did that, God would bless her government. If not, he wouldn't.

We moved on to Hyde Park. The police had told us that PA for music would not be allowed and that no meeting could be conducted there. As the 55,000 streamed into Hyde Park, an open-backed lorry and one microphone was all that was allowed. The triumvirate encouraged people to sit on the grass, eat their packed lunches, share them with those who had not brought a lunch and pray for London. The idea was that as they finished their lunch, they would go off to different parts of London and pray.

But that was not what happened. The entire 55,000 parked themselves in Hyde Park! They ate their lunch, shared with those without and prayed in groups. There was no programme arranged on the back of the lorry. No such programme had been allowed permission. Songs were sung, in an ad hoc, spontaneous fashion. Occasional bits of news were given by Roger, John Noble, Jean Darnall and myself, as to numbers and the reception at 10 Downing Street.

Still they didn't go. Police arrived. The senior officer in charge of the police operation was asked to come and give a few words. He thanked the crowd for their orderliness, good behaviour and happy atmosphere. He wished all such crowds were this well-behaved. He got a rousing cheer and then prayers from those assembled.

The march meeting at the Embankment had started at 11 am. By noon it had set off for Hyde Park. The first few hundred from the snake-like event had arrived way before 2 pm. At 4 pm, most were still there. This was twice the size of the Nationwide Festival of Light held in Trafalgar Square in 1971. We knew God was doing something very special with his people.

We had known when we handed in our letter at 10 Downing Street that Mrs Thatcher was not there, but we had not been told where she was. On our return home, we learned from a television report that she was in Scotland. She made a controversial speech to the Church Assembly there. This was the very day almost 60,000 evangelical Christians marched down Whitehall, probably the first time that had happened. She went on television to say that what the country needed was Christian ethics, morals and values. It was an amazingly well-timed speech and one her opponents took exception to.

Back in the House of Commons, for the next two or three weeks, especially at Prime Minister's question time, her Christian stand and the attack continued. Researchers and speech-writers scoured dictionaries and talked to Bible-believing Christians. Material was amassed. Neil Kinnock, a self-confessed agnostic, if not an atheist, hurled Bible verses across the floor of the House of Commons. Mrs Thatcher hurled different ones back. The teachings of Jesus got more exposure outside of the 'God slot' over those three weeks than in the previous thirty years!

We were now caught up in something which showed there was a massive vacuum of dynamic Christian leadership in the country, and a massive ground swell of people at grass-root level who are looking to be led. The 1987 May event had been hard work; there were no models—we had to be the model and make the model. But the turn-out and response of goodwill among new church and denominational evangelicals had been quite remarkable.

The Westminster event in May of 1988 had created double the expected turn-out. If the events following the City march of 1987 had surprised us, the events following the 1988 Westminster day were more surprising. Mrs Thatcher had not made the sort of statement she did that night on national television at any time in her nine years of power. Nor did she make such statements in the following two years.

At the close of the 1988 event, I walked over to Jean Darnall, one of the Council of Reference who had been on the platform in the Embankment. I put my arms around her and whispered in her ear, 'Lights across the nation indeed, Jean.' Jean broke down and wept.

Jean had received a vision she believed was from the Lord. It was of little lights appearing all over the nation.

They began to link up until the land was ablaze. But this was not in 1990. This was in 1970!

Through Fountain Trust, the Nationwide Festival of Light, *Come Together* and individual personalities, renewal had come to the shores of Great Britain in the early seventies. There was a great deal of fruit to show for those days, but it was limited and the renewal movement levelled off by the late seventies. Acts 86 had drawn around 10,000 people together within denominational Christianity. It was a noble attempt at creating a forum to encourage believers in denominational churches. Thank God for that! But so many went back to churches that were open to the gospel but closed to the Holy Spirit, or closed to both.

Something else was needed, something that would accelerate the process of revival. Roger, Lynn and I, with our colleagues, continued to pray and had a growing vision for a nationwide March for Jesus. We hardly knew what we were doing from one year to the other. It was hoped that in September 1989 perhaps twelve major cities would stage their own event, linked by satellite or landline. There would be a programme with prayers for the nation.

As before, these would not be marches and prayers against issues but for issues. They would be for light, for life, for families, for the marginalised. This event was not intended to be merely an expression of triumphalism or an alternative to social action and getting one's hands dirty. This would be an expression of multitudes of grass-root initiatives all over the country, with young people, the elderly, the unemployed, AIDS sufferers and the homeless. We knew we would be charged with triumphalism, but only by those who refused to acknowledge, or were ignorant of, grass-root activities in localities.

Saturday September 16th was set to be the date for

the nationwide March for Jesus. But the twelve intended centres eventually grew to forty-five. A printed programme of prayers and songs stopped the forty-five from becoming purely localised. The majority took the programme, as they did the landline link (in effect the same as satellite).

All created their own pre-programme of music, participants and prayers. Then the landline was opened for thirty minutes. Around 200,000 Christians were harmonised in prayer and purpose for the nation. The weather was mixed. In some places, the sun was shining and people stood with responsive attentiveness. In other places, it was pouring with rain and thirty minutes of listening to messages from Belfast, Edinburgh, Birmingham, Cardiff and London was a test of patience.

They prayed for the United Kingdom, they prayed for Europe and they shared plans for the future. Another nationwide March for Jesus, but this time 'Where You Live', took place in September 1990, with evangelistic initiatives in the evening shaped up by local churches and ministries. In 1991 there would be a similar event, but this time with the focus of evangelism and social action, for a specific period of time, perhaps a week. It would be named Challenge 2000—Discipling a Whole Nation.

Then I announced over the landline link that in 1992 we would be moving to something special. 'We are expecting that in every capital city of every European nation, East and West, there will be a major March for Jesus on the same day.' On my way home I remarked to Anona, 'We must be mad, we can't even get into some of those countries!'

There was no way we could have known about events that would take place after September 1989. In November, the Berlin Wall came down; in December Romania's Nikolae Ceaucescu was taken out and shot—

on Christmas Day which celebrates the birth of the Man
he didn't believe in. Ceaucescu made everyone work on
that day. He would not allow it to be celebrated. Since
then, the heart and face of Europe has been undergoing
continual change.

Numbers grow each year. In 1987, 15,000 marched in
the City of London; 55,000 in 1988 in Westminster;
200,000 in forty-five centres all over the United Kingdom
in 1989. Over 200,000 took to the streets, and many
evangelised their areas in the autumn of 1990.

But it is not just a question of increasing numbers: the
media coverage resulting from this growing impact is at
last beginning to happen. The day after the 1990 March
for Jesus, Ishmael and his church were the subject of
ITV's *Morning Worship*, while in the evening *Songs of
Praise* tied in with March for Jesus live from Leeds
Castle in Kent. The programme was most notable for
the breakdown of the outside broadcast system, so
viewers were treated with a repeat of Spring Harvest
1989 instead! We were screened two weeks later.

Many of these plans and thoughts came out of fellowship and prayer, and further new ideas were to emerge
as a result of the time Roger, Lynn and I spent together
in the Pioneer office. It had been John Presdee's idea to
march through the City, and mine to go through
Westminster. The concept of the nationwide March for
Jesus came from the steering group. March for Jesus
Where You Live was back to me, though the idea of a
nationwide prayer meeting afterwards in Westminster
Hall, addressed by Larry Lea, was Laurence
Singlehurst's.

At the end of a meeting, and after a little food and
drink, we were allowing our hearts and minds to wander.
'What if we launched a new initiative,' I mused, 'to reach
the nation with the gospel by the year 2000?'

We looked at each other knowingly. The existing

relationships, networks and goodwill would allow March
for Jesus to be a catalyst. We ourselves could not
possibly direct the strategy. All the living body of Christ
would have to be involved in being good news, sharing
good news, preaching good news, and strategically
planting churches wherever possible. Graham Kendrick's
songs and Steve Clifford's management skills have been
invaluable. Their investment is seeing an extraordinary
return!

We sowed the seeds for evangelism in the 1989
programme. We prayed a corporate prayer of commitment to be and to communicate the good news. 'I don't
imagine for one moment that many people took us too
seriously,' I commented afterwards. 'There were many
words, many ideas and many seeds sown throughout
that time.'

But from that moment on, serious plans were under
way to link evangelism and social action with the 1990
project, enlarge in 1991 and broaden in 1992 across
Europe.

The Church of England, quite separately, launched
their own Decade of Evangelism. Other denominations
worked with the idea. The Assemblies of God and Elim
churches began to work out church-planting strategems.
The Baptists looked the most hopeful to renew existing
churches and plant new ones.

At our request, MARC Europe began to put the
entire nation on computer. They started to track evangelistic events, the people reached, the numbers
responding, and those who related into the church.
This initiative was never triumphalist, dosed with a lot
of charismatic rhetoric. March for Jesus leaders had
been leading growing churches, launching social action
initiatives and promoting charismatic orthodoxy for
over twenty years.

It was foreseen early on that there would be major

parts of Britain unevangelised. Groups would need to move and plant churches if existing churches could not be revitalised.

There was suspicion, as various church leaders heard about these initiatives. March for Jesus had a broad Council of Reference and a magazine, *Forward*, which kept people informed of developments. There had been several private and two public consultations with evangelical leaders. But not all could make them. Some lived in distant parts of the country and certainly couldn't come down to London.

A few church leaders even spoke against March for Jesus quite publicly. This was not based on any fellowship or discussion with the main leaders of March for Jesus. At times I felt like Lord Clive of India, who had at one time owned our home in Esher. He died in 1774, aged forty-nine. He declared in a parliamentary cross-examination in 1773, 'By God, Mr Chairman, at this moment of time I stand astonished at my own moderation!' I was not renowned for moderation, though I amazed myself as to how I kept silent publicly, when tunnel-minded church leaders put us on the rack for wanting to see Great Britain evangelised!

True, in certain areas there may have been triumphalism. But certain parts of the body of Christ had not even heard of March for Jesus, despite its growing numbers and influence. There might well be others who felt left out because they had not been invited onto the Council of Reference or drawn into a forum of consultation. But there was no need to denigrate this initiative of prayer and evangelism publicly or privately. To me, it was like setting fire to a house in order to gain the attention of the builders.

So, Challenge 2000 was born, with the aim of reaching everybody in the nation, 'over and over again' with the gospel. Lynn Green came up with the idea of encouraging churches to reach everyone in their areas in five different ways:

a piece of gospel literature

face-to-face, one-to-one presentation of the gospel

an invitation to a specialist event

through something read, heard or seen in the secular media

an event in the home, using a video, an audio-tape or something similar.

So what is March for Jesus all about? Prayer? Yes! Getting the praise of our God out onto the streets where it can be seen and heard? Yes again! (Not to be confused with self-righteous prayers we want everyone else to see, for self-satisfaction. Remember, the early church had no churches to meet in. It was homes, occasional halls or the open air, such as Solomon's Portico!)

But March for Jesus and Challenge 2000 are more than prayer, more than visibility; they're even more than evangelism and social action. We are praying, marching, and expecting for nothing short of revival! With all of the wonderful initiatives in this Decade of Evangelism, we will never get the job of evangelising the nation done in our lifetime without revival.

Is revival God's sovereign act? Well, it is not unrelated to expectation and prayer. During the nationwide March for Jesus, Graham Kendrick and Ian Traynar led two teams and walked and prayed throughout the entire length of the land. In 1990, during March for Jesus Where You Live, Graham led another team from the Welsh coast across to the English east coast, praying for the nation as they went.

But if revival is a sovereign work of God, should we pray, plan and expect it to happen? Could it even come and we miss it? Unthinkable? It has happened before. Why? Because God came in ways that the praying body were not expecting. The reaction of the Jews to the birth, life and ministry of Jesus is a classic example of an apparently orthodox biblical faith missing the most strategic, historic breakthrough. Revivals even in Britain were preceded by praying people who then carried on praying long after the revival had gone. They did not believe that what they saw was the revival God wanted, or initiated.

If revival breaks out in the United Kingdom, the first opponents will be evangelicals, conservative and even charismatic evangelicals, who want to see things 'done decently and in order', and will not be able to equate the wildfire with the Intelligent Fire, hilarity with holiness, or emotionalism with the tears of God.

How could they?

Chapter 11

New Directions

Anona and I had been happily married for over twenty-three years. Paul, twenty-one, worked for the Historic Royal Palaces Agency. Simon, nineteen, was an accomplished landscape-gardener. Jonathan, twelve, was getting interested in model classic cars!

Our home in Esher had no live-in friends, long-term lodgers or paying guests. Norman and Sheila had gone to live in Virginia Beach, USA. Sheila co-hosted *The 700 Club* with Pat Robertson, surely the most prestigious of all the Christian programmes shown coast to coast. Watched by several million people a day, she was then given her own programme, *Heart to Heart*. At times it topped *The 700 Club* ratings. There was plenty of communication by phone, letter or by occasional personal visits—but Sheila and Norman had found their own home and a special role in America.

The church in Cobham continued to grow. They had moved from being a cruise liner to a battleship. Every time they filled St Andrew's School hall (the largest hall in Cobham), they planted out. Duncan and Jan Weir now headed up the church-plant in Farnham. Edwyn and Sue Pelly returned to Cobham to broaden the leadership team. Mick and Liz Ray led the Molesey Christian Fellowship nearby. Roger and Angie Stephenson continued with the demanding, but highly successful church-plant in Tooting. Euwan and Kate McKenzie, plus others from local churches, planted out in Wandsworth. Martin Scott, who had led the Cobham church for four years, was overseeing churches across South and West of London and beyond. He was 'cracking the Leatherhead nut', as I often called it. Even Wesley gave up on the area! They were starting a fellowship there, and saw conversions at most meetings.

Our bimonthly prayer events in Tolworth were attracting around 1,000 people and our bimonthly celebration events attracted a similar number. Up to 200 leaders met quarterly for prayer and for teaching from R. T. Kendall, Barney Coombs, Stuart Bell, Roger Forster, John Noble and others. New churches were being added to the network in our area.

Kevin Allan led a network of churches in Pioneer Solent. Roger Ellis did the same in Pioneer South. Stuart Bell had his own Ground Level team and cared for a growing network from the Humber to the Wash and beyond. Other key leaders within Pioneer seemed to be doing well. Each was seeing the kind hand of God upon their lives, families and churches. Things were looking relatively healthy. National ministries such as Ishmael, Pete Gilbert, Noel Richards and Mike Morris were growing in faith, love and usefulness.

Danny Smith of the Jubilee Campaign was overworked but having his prayers answered. So was Dr Patrick Dixon of ACET, the AIDS initiative. The March for Jesus story unfolded without major problems, despite its national spread.

We were aware that the Enemy wanted to destroy the Pioneer work, perhaps knock out one or two of its regions, or spoil some of its initiatives. Interface was an event which attracted over 1,000 teenagers, in several centres, for a dynamic approach to the Christian life. There was strong biblical teaching and a lot of fun. The long-term (year-long) and short-term (summer holidays) TIE Teams (Training in Evangelism) was one of the most successful projects we'd launched. Hundreds were coming to faith through their work. A new breed of evangelists was emerging.

New opportunities and relationships were on the horizon: singer/songwriter Caroline Bonnet; songwriter and worship leader Jo King; Mike Puscy, now in Newport, Gwent brought his church into the Pioneer network, a remarkable development in the light of working with him at Capel almost twenty years previously; Ishmael had trained up Richard Hubbard, who now had his own growing, influential children's family ministry in his own right; Ian White, a wonderful singer/songwriter, best known for his psalms put to music, was a friend of Stuart Brunton's. The Pioneer team had worked with him for several years. Singer Nanette Wellman was related to Adrian and Pauline Hawkes' churches in North London. There were others.

At times we were tired and exhausted. But it was all worth it.

We'd lost a couple of team members, one in the summer of 1986 and, sadly, another in the summer of 1988. We remained friendly with them both, but they were a significant loss nevertheless. However, things felt good and healthy. So we were quite unprepared for what happened next. We were feeling cautiously optimistic.

I was extremely busy. Apart from my responsibilities with the family, our home, and the Pioneer team, I also acted in an advisory capacity to Danny Smith and Dr Patrick Dixon and had regular meetings with Roger Forster, Lynn Green and Steve Clifford. Throughout

1990 I spent three weeks in New Zealand, a week in Malta, several days in West and East Germany, several more in Switzerland, and had numerous long weekends away at large celebration events and leaders' conferences. I was privileged to be a main platform speaker at Spring Harvest and the Grapevine conference in Lincoln, and fulfilled a special weekend in Dundee with our friends Stuart and Marie Brunton. I was having to turn down as many invitations as I was accepting.

And the point of all this information? Life was full, rewarding, if at times demanding and a little frustrating—but I wouldn't have changed it for anything. But God had other plans!

The month was May 1990. It was before the prophetic controversy surrounding John Wimber and Paul Cain. Norman Barnes, based in Essex, was Director of the already mentioned Links International. Two of his friends, Dale and Jean Gentry, were in the country. Would Cobham have them? They were only going to his church in Chadwell Heath and Pioneer-related River Church in Marlow-Maidenhead, led by Alistair Bullen. Martin Scott discussed it with the rest of the Cobham leaders and we went ahead. We trusted Norman and his judgement.

Dale turned out to be a quiet, somewhat conservative, neatly dressed man in his late forties or early fifties. Jean was an attractive, charming, perceptive individual. They spoke to our discipleship group. The teaching was good, and his words and prophecies for individuals seemed accurate. A specially invited group of ninety attended the seminars on the Saturday, when both the level of teaching and prophetic ministry went up a notch or two in our estimation. Up to then, our response was simple. If he was back in a couple of years, we would have him. Then came Sunday night.

St Andrew's School hall was jammed to the walls, and it was literally standing-room only. A strong time of praise preceded his talk. He knew virtually nothing of us. 'This church has a mind-set,' he began, 'a mind-set which God wants to break.' He continued, 'I want to bring the scripture relating to Peter when he was sent to the house of Cornelius.' He told the story well. 'Not me, Lord, not me—you've got the wrong person. We don't do it that way here.'

Some of my leadership team caught each other's eyes. What on earth can he mean? The Cobham Fellowship was built on strong biblical principles. But we had a great degree of flexibility. Cobham was one of the first to bring women into leadership and then eldership. We'd met on Sundays, at times we had met on Thursdays, and for one period we had no public meetings at all! We were flexible! We believed in what I call 'dynamic church', along with dynamic theology, dynamic relationships and a dynamic approach to the Scriptures. What was this 'mind-set'?

Dale continued, 'I see thousands of people becoming Christians in this area—thousands.' He went on to explain that they would be coming from all over the area. He explained this would happen quickly and that we should look for a 'facility'. He underlined the importance of the entire church being involved in continual prayer. We gulped! We'd already got a model, church-planting, all across the area, peppering South and West of London with churches. Others in the various Pioneer areas and networks were doing as well. Mega-church didn't quite fit with our plans!

He went on to explain to the church that their vision would have to die, it was not big enough. Some remarkable miracles would be performed, touching the lives of the influential, people he called 'movers and shakers'. He proclaimed that a new spirit of boldness would come upon the Cobham church. What happened then we've not seen in twenty years of church life together.

As he was finishing his talk, numerous people began to move to the front. As Dale and Jean prayed with individuals for no more than a few seconds, one after another collapsed on the floor. At times there were three or four people piled on top of each other. A twenty-one-year-old girl, who had been converted for just a few days, from a totally godless background, was standing on her chair with her arms in the air shouting out 'Jesus! Jesus! Jesus!'

The following night, seventy leaders from the area who relate to the Pioneer team, came together. He told the assembled group, 'Your vision must die,' and went on to explain that God wanted to do something much bigger than we have ever asked or thought of.

On his final night, the elders and full-time leaders who relate to Cobham were together. He reiterated that thousands were going to come to Christ, that the influential would find salvation and get counsel here in the area and in London. He explained that in his vision, he saw a whole orchestra, classical concerts and people in evening dress. This would be accompanied by miraculous signs and wonders. He went on to explain he saw the word 'hall'. He wasn't sure whether it was a full word or a partial word, but felt it was an important word. He then went on to prophesy over each individual leader and their partners—some he'd never spoken to. The accuracy was quite remarkable. The prophecies were transcribed. For two and a half weeks we prayed, talked, laughed and cried over them.

It was now the beginning of June. Barney Coombs shared in the last part of our Pioneer team-day and spoke to almost 200 leaders in the evening. He was excellent. My personal assistant, Rob Dicken, came up to me at the close of the meeting and handed me an

Ordnance Survey map of the area. 'I don't know why I'm giving you this,' he explained nervously. 'I was in Farrant's the newsagents in Cobham and I simply felt the Lord ask me to give this to you.' Barney came back for some supper with Noel and Trish. I looked at the map, shrugged my shoulders and took it over to the office the next morning and put it in my 'to be filed' tray.

Next day I went to the full-time elders' meeting. We went through the prophecies again, laughing and crying. We sensed there were three keys. The first was that something was going to happen in the area that we need to prepare for and for which we should seek a 'facility'. The second was to do with the word 'hall', and we already had a good idea what that meant. The third had to do with me, the media, and fronting this new phase. Most significantly, he spoke of a father-figure who he wasn't sure was in place. The only person it could be was John Noble. I had looked to several men over the last twenty years, at different times and for different things, but the only one I could consider a father-figure was John.

So now what? With that, Nigel Day brought out an identical Ordnance Survey map from his brief-case! The reason? Trish Richards, the day before Dale had arrived, had received a vision of Martin's wife, Sue, addressing a large meeting in an aircraft hangar! We weren't looking for aircraft hangars then!

'I've found two aircraft hangar sites,' Nigel told us. He spread the map on the table. The first one had been demolished, it turned out. The other was on the British Aircraft Corporation site. It had once been the home of Brooklands runway and Brooklands racing-track. Virtually the whole site had been demolished and a brand-new high-tech industrial park was being erected by Trafalgar House.

'Having made investigations, I went and had a look at it,' Nigel told us. 'It's a large aircraft hangar with car-parking for about 400 cars. Three days later I went back, and guess what? "To Let" signs have just gone up!' We could possibly get up to 2,000 in the building and there were all sorts of other offices and facilities on site.

As I looked at the Ordnance Survey map, I noticed something. Not one house on St George's Hill Estate was named. There were hundreds of houses in the up-market setting, the place where so many 'movers and shakers' lived. But I spied one, Blue Barn Farm. I shook my head in amazement. A publisher, Paul Williams, had recently moved into Cobham to be a part of the fellow-ship and had purchased Blue Barn Farm. It consisted of a large barn that could take a good hundred people for a social gathering. The house was built around it in large grounds. The property backed onto the aircraft hangar! Other than Cliff Richard, he was the only person we knew on the entire estate.

Three months previously, Paul and his wife, Amanda, came to tell me they were thinking of buying the property. I remarked that it was out of Cobham, and certainly not within walking distance of the rest of the people in Cobham Fellowship. But I felt good about it nevertheless. As they were leaving I found myself saying, 'Once you are in the property, you're going to find something in the house or on the land which is going to make your move there fall into place.' Paul trusted me, and asked what such a thing could be. I replied, 'I haven't got a clue.' Now I knew.

Trish came to see the aircraft hangar which had doors all along the front, just as she saw it in her vision. She had seen it in its finished and completed state. 'As far as I can tell, this is the one,' she said.

We were reeling! First there were the prophecies for

the area, London, and myself. Then the aircraft hangar, which was derelict but only a few days later, to let. We then found that the only property on St George's Hill Estate owned by a member of the Cobham Christian Fellowship—purchased just a few weeks previously—actually backed onto the hangar. And God had given us a word about it! Could more happen? It was about to.

My leaders began to negotiate with the company who owned the property and the local planners. I knew we'd also have to address the St George's Hill Residents Association. The Diggers, radical evangelicals in the Cromwellian period, used St George's Hill as a base. 'Do me a brief history of the Diggers,' I said to David Taylor, one of our elders and a local historian.

A few days later he phoned. 'You had better sit down—you're not going to believe this!' He seemed incredulously bemused. 'I've just had a phone call from Dr Christopher Hill. He's asked if I will write a book with him. That's like being in Cobham Football Club and being asked to get ready to play in the FA Cup Final at Wembley!'

I paused. 'What's the book about?'

He laughed. 'He's asked me to write a book with him on the Diggers!'

I then went to Switzerland. In Berne, at the final meeting—a very special meeting—a man who couldn't speak a word of English spoke through an interpreter. He had received a dream about the meeting-place we were in. 'It's too small,' he explained, through the interpreter. He went on to say he saw a terrorist or gang leader giving his testimony on a large stage, in front of 2,000 people.

Through the interpreter, I asked, 'Is it made of brick with windows, wooden ...'

He interrupted: 'No, it is made of iron, it has an oval

roof and it is black.' That described the aircraft hangar perfectly!

So what of the 'father-figure'? We contacted John and Christine Noble of Team Spirit, explained the prophecies to them and met two weeks later for breakfast. Despite the absurdity of John moving from Essex to Surrey, especially as he leads the Team Spirit network of churches and initiatives, they both felt this was of God. The result was that John and Christine would 'flow out of' my vision, but I am submitting much of what I'm doing to him for his fatherly counsel, wisdom and insight.

A new era had begun. The Intelligent Fire was about to lighten the darkness of 'thousands'.

Epilogue
Paul Cain's Prophecy

In July 1990 I was one of around a thousand leaders who attended the 'Prophecy' Conference led by John Wimber and a team mainly drawn from Kansas City Fellowship. The controversy surrounding the Clifford Hill review of David Pytches' book *Some Said It Thundered*, and several private letters to leaders from Clifford Hill, engaged me in both public and private debate.

I was most unhappy about the so-called review. It was Clifford Hill's personal perspectives on the book, but also on the Kansas City Fellowship and several of the personalities involved there. I came to the conclusion that there must be a better way of dealing with concerns than this public forum.

I had contacted John Wimber with regard to my own perspectives on David Pytches' book, Clifford Hill's article and several private letters, assuring him of my support and that of many I was working with. That there were excesses and areas that needed adjustment with some of the leaders in KCF was not in question. But if we all published inflammatory articles about brothers in leadership with whom we did not agree over issues such as the charismas of the Spirit, prophecy, accountability, Keep-Sunday special campaign, being a part of a local church (which many well-known leaders are not!) apostolic ministry and Calvinism, there would hardly be a friendship left in leadership circles!

Over a sandwich lunch, I updated John on my perspectives and that of other colleagues I work with. The next day I expressed how well many of us thought he had handled himself in a non-reactionary fashion, actually promoting a Clifford Hill book saying it's probably 'the best' on the subject. He thanked me for our friendship and was in tears as we stood in the garden with Sandy Millar, the vicar of Holy Trinity Brompton, who was hosting the conference.

I was asked if I would like to talk with some of the Kansas City Prophets and receive prayer or prophecy. After consideration I declined their kind offer. I felt I had received so many prophecies from Dale Gentry, there was so much revelation around, I wasn't looking for more. If God had something for me he would bring it my way. He did!

On the last night John invited me to his hotel for supper. Clive Calver joined us, together with John's wife Carol. I encouraged Clive to talk about himself, the Evangelical Alliance, and his own perspectives on recent prophetic issues. We then went into the dining room where John asked me what was happening with myself. I told him about Dale Gentry's prophecies, the area 'hangar' vision, the spread into London, personal prophecies for me with regard to the media and the need of the 'father figure'. I explained that John and Christine Noble were, as a result of these prophecies, moving to Cobham along with members of their family. So that we would know these things were of God we also felt he had given us tokens of his intent. I told him the story of Nathan with regard to the 'tremendous move of God among young people'. Despite being in a public restaurant both John and Carol wept as I got to the final line of the story, that the parents had given their son Nathan to me for ministry training.

They left for the meeting and I stayed on to talk with Clive. Mike Bickle from the Kansas City Fellowship came across and asked if I had a son named Jonathan. It seemed that Paul Cain, who had been sitting several tables away, had asked who was having supper with John and Carol, and whether I had a son called Jonathan. He had a word for him.

The restaurant emptied, but Clive and I stayed, expressing our appreciation for John and Carol and the time they had given us. We wandered down to Holy Trinity to find the worship had finished, and John was rounding off his talk. Paul Cain came to the microphone. He gave two or three prophetic words for individuals.

He then called out my name, explaining I had 'something to do with these meetings'. He began: 'I have an awesome word from the Lord for you—I have come all the way over here to give it—and I feel like it would honour the Lord to give it publicly.' He continued, 'The Lord is going to help you through every controversy in your life—he's going to help you to be established, show you his geographic will. In your heart you know you are not in the geographic will of God right now. I think that means something about the building or the gathering place.

'I see an old metal building—does that mean anything to you?' At this point elders and leaders from Cobham and several within the Pioneer network shouted out in shock and clapped—to the astonishment of others who obviously had no clue about the relevance of these words. He went on to say that the Lord was overseeing the project, the Lord's money would not be wasted and that it would be a 'grace package'.

He enquired, 'You may be a controversial figure—I

don't know.' At this point there was uproarious laughter from the entire conference.

He concluded that he saw there were five people in my family, that I had a son called 'Jo, Nathan, Jonathan.' Prophecies concerning Jonathan's future were given. The prophecy told me not to worry about my family, and that God had put them in a 'grace package'.

Then he saw a woman called 'Ann Stevens?' but then added, 'No, it's Ann and she is with a tall strong man, her husband. I see the face of Steven. You two are going to work together.' This must refer to Steve and Ann Clifford, who are two of our closest friends. Although we work closely on March for Jesus, TIE Teams and youth projects, there are many other pulls on Steve's time with Spring Harvest, the EA Executive and other forums. It was not inconceivable that within a short while Steve would be working with lots of others as well as me, or even not at all. This was not in Steve's heart, but it was a clear prophetic word as to where his commitments lay.

I was invited back for supper to meet Paul Cain and others, but as I had my car at Esher railway station I declined, as I was totally dependent on public transport. As I was walking out with several friends from Cobham, including Martin Scott, Paul Cain and a group from KCF passed by the other way. I walked over, put out my hand to thank him for the words, and he responded, 'Oh—it's you.' He then pulled out a pack of beige cards in his pocket, one of which had my name on it.

What he hadn't read out were words on the card that had to do with 'crowds—marching'. And then at the bottom he put 'Johnathan' in joined-up writing and then as a separate word in capital letters NATHAN. Under Nathan he'd put 'adopted???' He had no idea of the Nathan story or that he was going to meet me again. He should have left England without ever seeing me again.

It was another confirmation that one era had been closed and another was about to begin. What fights, controversies and tests of faith were up ahead were not clear. They will probably warrant another book!

*'God makes his angels winds
and his servants flames of fire.'*
Hebrews 1:7 (GNB)

Pioneer

The Pioneer team send out a quarterly magazine containing news of its network of churches, training programmes for leaders and evangelists, conferences and news on a wider level. The magazine is free but donations are appreciated to cover costs.

If you would like more details about the Jubilee Campaign, ACET, or March for Jesus, you should write to the address below enclosing a stamped addressed envelope—we will do all we can to supply you with what you need.

A large list of audio and video tapes of Gerald Coates' ministry is also available. Send a large SAE and we will do the rest.

Pioneer
PO Box 79c
Esher
Surrey
KT10 9LP

 **Kingsway Publications**

Kingsway Publications publishes books to encourage spiritual values in the home, church and society. The list includes Bibles, popular paperbacks, more specialist volumes, booklets, and a range of children's fiction.

Kingsway Publications is owned by The Servant Trust, a Christian charity run by representatives of the evangelical church in Britain, committed to serve God in publishing and music.

For further information on the Trust, including details of how you may be able to support its work, please write to:

The Secretary
The Servant Trust
1 St Anne's Road
Eastbourne
East Sussex BN21 3UN
England